INTEGRATED MARKETING COMMUNICATION

STRATEGY, BRAND EXPERIENCE, AND TOUCHPOINTS

Dino Villegas

Texas Tech University

Kendall Hunt
publishing company

Cover image © Shutterstock.com

www.kendallhunt.com
Send all inquiries to:
4050 Westmark Drive
Dubuque, IA 52004-1840

Copyright © 2019 by Kendall Hunt Publishing Company

ISBN 978-1-5249-5884-8

Published in the United States of America

Contents

Initial Words

I read my first marketing book very early in my youth, when I was waiting in my father's office after a long school day. There weren't many other means of distraction so I started reading what turned out to be my life-long passion. I was impressed by the idea of strategies, understanding people and competition. I was seduced by the stories of Coca-Cola® vs. Pepsi® and fascinated by how marketers positioned brands.

Since then, I have witnessed many changes in Marketing—first as a practitioner and then as an academic. Technology has changed, theories have evolved and society is always moving. In this book, I wanted to address some of these changes from a practical point of view.

This book is meant to guide your learning process, spark your curiosity and generate constructive discussions. It will hopefully inspire you to know more as those old books did for me. This is why I planned this book to be a short text that goes straight to the essential elements of the theory and practice of IMC. This book is a starting point but not the ending word.

To add interactivity, you will find two distinct elements that will support your learning:

1. *Application Exercise:* These are exercises in which you can reflect and/or apply the knowledge discussed in the chapters.
2. *Recommended Material*: The book recommends many readings and videos; you will find a link to this material, divided by chapter, at this site: www.imcstrategy.com

I hope you enjoy reading this book as much as I did writing it. If you have any comments or wish to discuss it, please email me at dino.villegas@ttu.edu.

This book would not have been possible without the curious questions of and the discussions I have had with every one of my students; thanks to you all. Special thanks to my colleagues at the Rawls College of Business and to everyone involved in this project at Kendall Hunt for their support.

Finally, I want to thank my wife, Coni and my sons, Lucas and Pascual, for their unconditional love and also my parents for always inspiring me to be the best that I can be.

Chapter 1
Introduction to Integrated Marketing Communication

The world is changing. Marketing Communications is changing with the world.

© Zapp2Photo/Shutterstock.com

In this chapter we will discuss the most important issues related to Integrated Marketing Communication (IMC), starting with relevant definitions, then moving on to changes in context, and finally, proposing a framework for IMC that will serve as the overall guide for this book.

Learning Objectives for This Chapter:

- Discuss the concept of IMC.
- Define "marketing."
- Illustrate the concept of communication and its application for marketing.
- Identify changes in the world and how they affect IMC.
- Develop a framework for IMC.

IMC Definitions

The concept of Integrated Marketing Communication has been described in various literature using different approaches. To begin our exploration of the concept, we will first define what we mean when we talk about marketing. Once this is clear, we will move to the understanding of communication as a phenomenon on its own as well as how it defines IMC. Finally, in this sub-section, we will discuss more fully what we mean by "integrated."

So, What Is Marketing?

If you are reading this book, there is a pretty good chance that this is not your first marketing reading. You may have read other books on the subject or taken classes on it; however, I do believe that it is important to review what we know about the concept of marketing before we move forward. A clear definition or agreement on what we understand "marketing" to be is crucial to the understanding of IMC.

The American Marketing Association (AMA)—the most important professional association of marketing—has defined marketing as:

"...the activity, set of institutions, and processes for creating, communicating, delivering, and exchanging offerings that have value for customers, clients, partners, and society at large." (AMA, 2013)

As we can see, this definition includes all the activities (selling, research, or others) institutions (companies, agencies, or government), and processes (like planning) related to marketing. This definition also includes the creation, communication, and delivering of valuable offerings. So, marketing is not just about delivering a product but it also relates to how we listen to our customers to understand the value that they may need or want.

One of the key issues in this definition is the "communication" of these offerings; this is the part that we are interested in exploring in this book.

But, what does "communication" mean? And how does this relate to marketing?

What Is Communication?

So, when I said "communication," what was the first thing that came to your mind? Chances are you thought of a sender sending a message to a receiver and getting feedback. This model—proposed first in 1948 Claude Shannon's mathematical theory of communication and popularized in the book edited by Warren Weaver in 1948—or an adaptation of it, has been used as a framework to explain communication and specifically marketing communication in a diverse range of literature. We have seen variations of this model from different perspectives.

What do you imagine when you think of communication?

When this model is applied to marketing communication, it is easy to see how a brand can send a message to its target and then receive feedback as part of the behavior.

One of the concepts that is important in this model is the concept of noise; this is any type of barrier or distraction that keeps a message from being effectively delivered to a receiver. In marketing communication that can be anything from someone looking at his or her phone while a commercial is on TV to interpretations far from what the brand intended, as in the controversial Kendell Jenner commercial for Pepsi.

The linear model of communication, previously described, is however not exempt from criticism. Holm (2006), for example, said that this was an oversimplified model and defined communication as the process to achieve share

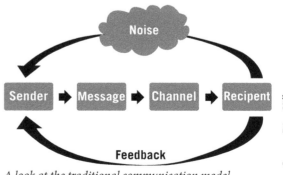

A look at the traditional communication model

meaning. Bowman and Targowski (1987) sustain that this model has been recognized as insufficient to describe the complexity of human communications.

It is, however, interesting to note that in communication theory, communication has been described from many perspectives, not just from a single linear view.

Communication has been defined as discourse, semiotics and symbols, experiences, and an information process, as well as interaction and influence to others (Craig, 1999).

The Spanish professor Rafael Alberto Perez described communication as one of the ways that we can interact with the world. As he explained, we can modify the world from a physical perspective (such as when I push a chair and the chair moves), from a chemical perspective (such as mixing different formulas), and from a symbolic perspective (such as when a symbol changes the way that someone sees the world). This symbolic interactionism is what we understand communication to be (Pérez, 2001).

So, communication is not just about sending a message, but, in my view, it is more about understanding and co-producing symbolic interactions and recognizing how those interactions affect others. The importance of the effect is already mentioned in the explanation of the mathematical model by Warren Weaver; he explains communication as " the procedure by which one mind may affect another" (Shannon & Weaver, 1963, p. 3).

In marketing, it's crucial that we understand, it is not just about the message, it is about the objective of the communication. Let me share an example that I use in class and that I heard from an old professor of mine many years ago.

© BLUR LIFE 1975/Shutterstock.com

Let's imagine that you are starting a new job. Your new boss has invited you to a dinner. You know (because someone informed you) that this boss likes people who are funny. Would you stand up in the middle of the dinner, raise your hand, and tell your boss: "Boss, I want to inform you that I'm very funny"? No you wouldn't.

So, what do you do?

You tell jokes; you act funny. You think to yourself, "What do I have to do so he thinks I'm funny." The message should be obvious through your actions.

The problem is that in marketing communications, many brands act as in the first example. They say things like "we are the best" or "we are the fastest" when they should be showing these things through examples.

Then, What Is IMC?

So, we have discussed the definition of marketing and the meaning of communication, but how do we define Integrated Marketing Communication? The AMA defined IMC as the:

> *"Planning process designed to assure that **all brand contacts** received by a customer or prospect for a product, service, or organization are **relevant** to that person and **consistent over time**."*

One important part of this definition is the concept of brand contacts. This refers to every point of contact the brand has with its customers. These touchpoints are the ones that create the customer brand experience. Brand contacts can be divided into Brand Identity Contacts, every contact between the brand and the brand stewards; and Brand Equity Contacts, every contact from the brand stewards to the actual customers (Madhavaram, Badrinarayanan & McDonald, 2005).

Another important element in this definition is consistency over time. Some authors have defined this as having one voice. This does not mean that we should give the exact same message in every platform, but instead that each message has to be consistent with the brand persona that we are communicating. Let's think, for example, of a brand such as Coca-Cola. In over 100 years, they have changed the advertising and the platforms that they use, but their message has always revolved around the concept of happiness.

As the IMC definition mentions, it is not enough for this voice to just be consistent; it has to also be relevant for the consumer. This is only possible with the right choice of segments and target markets as well as a good understanding of customer behavior, and the customer base's interests, values, and culture.

Every brand contact matters in the development of brand equity.

Along with understanding its customers, a brand must be able to maintain that one consistent voice. The IMC strategy has to fully consider Brand Identity Strategy, as every decision on IMC will impact brand equity (Madhavaram et al., 2005).

Marketing Integration

For many years, we used to define the operational process of marketing from the marketing mix of product, price, place, and promotion. Today we understand that these processes are integrated and changes on the price, for example, will impact the product perception from the customer. New technologies give us new opportunities. Selling on Facebook, for example, includes promotion as well as distribution.

Specifically, when we discuss "promotion" now, we understand that it includes far more than just promoting our products or services, and that every decision has to be integrated. Entering this new age of media, we cannot think that traditional advertising is isolated from what we do on social media or what our salespeople do. The use of agencies and communication consultants has to be part of a synergetic and integrated view; we cannot consider these to be separate efforts anymore.

The literature has distinguished four levels of integration in Integrated Marketing Communication (Kliatchko, 2008):

1. Tactical coordination of each marketing decision,
2. Decisions on the scope of marketing communications,
3. Decisions on the application of information technology in marketing communications,
4. and a financial and strategic integration, not just with marketing communications but with all brand decisions.

This integration is not easy. Organizational structures within companies, different objectives in each department, or simply a giving a low priority to the brand image can diminish the ability to coordinate this integration.

One of the main reasons to move from a "promotion" view to an IMC perspective is the big changes that we are seeing with technology and, more importantly, the use of this technology by the consumer (Table 1 summarizes some of the main changes).

Table 1 Some Changes that Affect IMC

- New technologies (social, mobile, and virtual)
- Integration of media platforms
- The ability to listen to the customer
- Power shifts and the co-creation of value
- From static marketing to an improv theater type of marketing (real-life decisions)
- Increase in brand competition and globalization
- Emphasis on measurable results and big data

Today, 69% of the public uses some type of social media (Perrin & Anderson, 2019), and social media is just one step into this vast new world. Interactive Web sites, blogs, social networks, smartphones, tablets, immersive VR, augmented reality, and all the other new technologies have led to an integration of the use of these media platforms with more traditional media.

Two studies from two of the biggest technology companies are fundamental to understanding this integrated use from the customer; these include the research on multi-screening from Google (C. Wojnicki, 2012) and a study from Microsoft (Microsoft Advertising, 2013).

Recommended Extra Reading:

- Cross-Screen Engagement, Microsoft Advertising
- The New Multi-Screen World Study, Google

Google maintains that most media interaction today is screen-based, and that smartphones are the backbone of this type of media use. According to this study, screens can be used in different contexts and situations; they specifically mention two types of what they call multi-screening. First, and the most used, is sequential usage; this is using one screen first (mobile, for example) and then a second one (a computer or tablet, for example) to continue the work or search. Because of this type of usage, Google recommends that companies enable customers to save progress between devices. The second type of usage is simultaneous; this is when two screen are used at the same time. In this case, what happens on one screen can trigger a behavior on a second screen (for example, looking at your phone for a product that you just saw on TV). According to Google, most of the time when someone is watching TV, a second screen is also being used.

In a similar study, Microsoft found four types of behaviors related to multi-screening:

a) Content grazing: The most common of the multi-screening, this is when consumers use two or more screens at the same time to access separate or unrelated content.

b) Investigative spider-webbing: Using two or more devices at the same time to gather additional information to enhance the primary screen experience. The consumer uses the second screen to research or complement the first.

c) Social spider-webbing: Sharing content while watching live events or television shows. While the user is watching content, he or she is also sharing reactions and opinions on a second screen, most likely in social media.

d) Quantum journey: Using different devices for a specific task. For example, a consumer can look up restaurants on a smartphone and later make a reservation using a tablet or notebook.

Most companies have become aware of this phenomenon, and how it affects consumers. Because of this, today's brands have to plan for multi-screening interaction; they cannot treat their various media platforms as different pieces of a puzzle, but as one cohesive image.

New technology has given us the ability to listen to the customer. The use of structured and unstructured data online, especially in social media, can help us monitor customer sentiment, map a network of or clusters of users that talk about our brand, and detect key topics important to our customers. But not everything is about numbers. Qualitative research techniques, such as netnography, can give us insights into the customer at a phenomenological and cultural level.

You may begin shopping for a product on your notebook and then finish buying it on your mobile phone; this is an example of sequential usage.

Simultaneous multi-screening is the new normal.

*In 2017 Burger King, using the interaction between devices, virtually hacked Google with a commercial that asked Google to define the Whopper. Suggested Video: **"Burger King Campaign Google Home"***

And this is not just a social media phenomenon. The Internet of Things, for example, provides us with a better understanding of the customer's use of our products. Companies like Caterpillar or Komatsu can connect and track their machinery and should be able to predict machine failure and adapt their innovation to the use of this machinery.

This new scenario has changed the way that companies produce value and the way consumers take part in it. Before, companies would create a product and then sell it to a distant consumer. The connection between the two was thin. Today, we have companies like Facebook or Twitter that provide an empty platform and the users are the ones who create as well asconsume the content on the platforms. This co-creation of value has passed way beyond the limits of technology-mediated products. Ikea is a great example of this customer/company partnership in value creation.

Facebook content is co-created among users.

Social media has also changed the way that we design and deliver brand messaging. Before the digital era, it took months to design an ad and then another few month to measure the results. Today, social media has made marketing communication similar to improv theater; we have a framework to use as a guide for brand creation, but the daily co-created—intentional and unintentional—content is what forges them.

All of this has been added to a fierce global competition where the numbers typically determine if a manager or a CEO will stay or step down. While in the past promotion performance efforts were difficult and sometimes impossible to measure, today's new technologies have solved that problem.

Community managers have to interact as the brand in real life with consumers.

Toward an IMC Framework

So, we have established that IMC is a coordinated effort that comes from brand strategy and will influence brand equity. This effort is impacted today by a series of changes that we previously described. But how does IMC work? What kinds of decisions do we have to make on a day to day basis?

IMC has four pillars (Kliatchko, 2008; Paul, 2017) that must be considered when we think about the IMC practice. The first is (a) the stakeholders. Specifically, we will ask ourselves about the customer (internal and external). How does the customer behave? How does he make buying decisions? How is her media consumption? The second is (b) the content of the communications, that is, the message and concepts to communicate. To understand this pillar, we need to add the comprehension of the brand and brand creation. Third is (c) the channel or platform mix that we are selecting. And finally, there's (d) the results. We will divide this pillar into two variables: the result objectives and the measuring of those results.

Book Structure

With these pillars in mind, we composed this book with the following ten chapters.

Chapter 1. Introduction to Integrated Marketing Communication. This chapter serves as an introduction and, at the same time, will define the most important concepts.

Chapter 2. Understanding Brand Context: Problems, Actors, and Customers. The second chapter focuses attention on pre-strategy—the understanding of the brand situation. This is one of the most important parts of any strategy and will be extremely relevant to the rest of the book.

Chapter 3. Segmentation, Targeting, and Positioning. Maybe one of the most important decisions in marketing, the segmentation-targeting-positioning process will be the framework of every IMC decision.

Chapter 4. Brand Creation and Development. This chapter deals with the brand—one of the most important assets for IMC—from choosing a brand name to deciding when and how to extend a brand.

Chapter 5. The IMC Mix Planning. After setting the brand and making all the strategic decisions, it is time to set our IMC mix. How to do it and the most important decisions to be made are discussed in this chapter.

Chapter 6. Advertising the Brand. We submerge in a review of traditional advertising, from designing the message to the different forms of media available, such as TV, radio, out-of- -home (outdoor) advertising, and print media.

Chapter 7. The Digital Brand. The main concepts of digital marketing and how to use it for IMC are discussed.

Chapter 8. The Social Brand. Social media marketing is discussed, from the different social media alternatives to the strategies and tactics that can be used in IMC.

Chapter 9. The Public Brand. This chapter covers how to deal with the media and public relations, how to use events for IMC, and what to do if the brand is under attack.

Chapter 10. Selling the Brand. IMC alternatives to convert to sales are discussed, from personal selling to direct marketing and sales promotions.

Application Exercise

Think about three of the brands that you use the most. How do the changes in this chapter apply to them?

Brands	Changes
1	
2	
3	

References

AMA. (2013). Marketing Definition. Retrieved from https://www.ama.org/AboutAMA/Pages/Definition-of-Marketing.aspx

Bowman, J. P., & Targowski, A. S. (1987). Modeling the Communication Process: The Map Is Not the Territory. *The Journal of Business Communication (1973), 24*(4), 21–34. doi:10.1177/002194368702400402

C. Wojnicki, A. (2012). *The New Multi-Screen World.* Retrieved from https://www.thinkwithgoogle.com/advertising-channels/mobile-marketing/the-new-multi-screen-world-study/

Craig, R. T. (1999). Communication theory as a field. *Communication Theory, 9*(2), 119–161.

Holm, O. (2006). Integrated marketing communication: From tactics to strategy. *Corporate Communications: An International Journal, 11*(1), 23–33.

Kliatchko, J. (2008). Revisiting the IMC construct: A revised definition and four pillars. *International Journal of Advertising, 27*(1), 133–160.

Madhavaram, S., Badrinarayanan, V., & McDonald, R. E. (2005). INTEGRATED MARKETING COMMUNICATION (IMC) AND BRAND IDENTITY AS CRITICAL COMPONENTS OF BRAND EQUITY STRATEGY: A Conceptual Framework and Research Propositions. *Journal of Advertising, 34*(4), 69–80. doi:10.1080/00913367.2005.10639213

Microsoft Advertising. (2013). Flamingo & Ipsos OTX, March 2013, n=3586 (Aus 499; Brazil 545; Canada 505; UK 1002; US 1035)

Paul, T. (2017). Implementing integrated marketing communications (IMC) through major event ambassadors. *European Journal of Marketing, 51*(3), 605–626. doi:10.1108/EJM-09-2015-0631

Pérez, R. A. (2001). *Estrategias de Comunicacion.* Madrid: Ariel.

Perrin, A., & Anderson, M. (2019). Share of U.S. adults using social media, including Facebook, is mostly unchanged since 2018. Retrieved from https://www.pewresearch.org/fact-tank/2019/04/10/share-of-u-s-adults-using-social-media-including-facebook-is-mostly-unchanged-since-2018/

Shannon, C. E., & Weaver, W. (1963). *The mathematical theory of communication:* University of Illinois press.

Chapter 2
Understanding Brand Context: Problems, Actors, and Customers

Your strategy begins with the research.

© Pixsooz/Shutterstock.com

A doctor should never recommend anything to a patient without first going through a diagnostic stage. IMC is no different. To make good marketing decisions, you need to understand the current brand situation and context, the potential problems and barriers, and the different actors involved, such as customers, competitors, and complementors.

Learning Objectives for This Chapter:

- Explain the relevance of research in IMC.
- Be able to decide on the right approaches for IMC research.
- Identify the different elements of social listening.
- Comprehend the concept of Voice of the Customer.

- Analyze and be able to map the customer journey,
- Identify consumer touchpoints.
- Recognize how customers make brand decisions.

Understanding First: Let the Research Lead Your Strategy

Imagine that KCBD News Channel, a local news channel in Lubbock Texas, has just asked you to develop an IMC strategy to grow their number of users/viewers by 20%.

What is the first thing that you do?

- Come up with a great idea to change the design of their app.
- Propose some new banners for their Website.
- Suggest a commercial during prime time on the TV channel where their program airs.

All of these can be good ideas, and I have heard most of them from my students when KCBD has asked them to solve this challenge in the past. However, all of them could also be wrong, or at least they shouldn't be the first thing that you do!

Why? Let's me explain.

The real secret to communication is listening and understanding others. You need to listen and understand their needs, wants, interest, dreams, and fears so you can speak from the counterpart perspective and not just from your own. This is true for communication with your friends, partner, or parents, and is also true for marketing communications.

Most communication problems occur because of listening problems. IMC is no different; listening to your customers is the first step to a successful campaign.

When you create an IMC strategy, what you are doing is generating a strategy that solves a specific problem to reach a goal. How you approach a brand that wants to grow 20% in users will be completely different if the problem that you are facing is an awareness problem or a brand association problem. If the problem is just awareness, the strategy could be as simple as having a better reach or introducing new touchpoints between the customer and the brand. However, if the problem is about the perception of the brand, then the solution can be far more complex. Understanding the problem should be the starting point of your strategy.

If you understand the customer, half of your job as a strategist is done…sure, this can be easier said than done. In IMC the most common problem that I have seen exhibited by students and professionals is jumping from a specific objective to a line of action without really understanding the context and the consumer.

Part of understanding the consumer involves gaining insight about symbols and signals used by your audience. For example, many experts claim that one of the many mistakes made in the 2017 Pepsi Campaign with Kendall Jenner was the lack of research and understanding of the audience as well as the possible lack of pre-testing with some of the groups involved in the message.

Here's something that we see frequently in international marketing. for example Coca-Cola was labeled as racist in Mexico after a campaign called #AbreTuCorazon or #openyourheart shows white kids handing Coca-Cola to local people in Oaxacan.

Even the big brands can make huge mistakes. Pepsi was under fire after a Kendall Jenner commercial, probably because of the lack of research and testing.

What Do We Look For?

Depending on the context, problem, objectives, and marketing strategy, you should look for different information using marketing research or secondary data. Some of the questions that you may want to explore are included below.

What Barriers Do We Have to Achieving Our IMC Objectives?

As we mentioned before, the understanding of the problem, barrier, or noise that might be affecting your achieving of your goal is going to be crucial to the development of your strategy.

In terms of the brand, there are at least three types of problems that you might discover. One problem is an **awareness problem**—that is, do the people on your target list know about your brand? For example, a relatively new product wants to grow its consumer base. Although the research can show that the product has good evaluations from current customers, the brand may only have a 10% awareness from their particular target.

Another problem could be about **brand knowledge**. For example, in the 90s Brita water filter had to educate consumers through TV commercials not just about the benefits of filtered water but also on how to use its products (Milliken, 2006).

Another issue that you could find is **brand association**. This can relate to positives or negatives. For example, brands can be perceived as innovative but risky or good quality but expensive. In addition, positive brand associations could actually be detrimental in reaching a proposed objective. For example, Bahama Buck's, a local company, is very well known for its shaved iced; however, it is so specialized that introducing new lines of products is a real challenge.

Other important questions that you should ask before working up a strategy are about your **competitors** and **complementors** (Brandenburger & Nalebuff, 1996). In a broad look at this, a competitor is any other offer or brand that targets the same needs or wants as your target segments. Another way to define "competition" is any offer that will reduce the value of your offer. In marketing communication, it is important to think about competition not only from an industry (producers) perspective, but also from a customer perspective. For example, Netflix sees the Fortnite game as (currently) its most important competitor not HBO (Tarrant, 2019), as they understand the market as a battle for users' screen time in general not just a competition against other streaming services.

Also important, and not always explored as it should, is the concept of complementors (Brandenburger & Nalebuff, 1996). This refers to every offer that will add value to your offer if used together. The analysis of complement products or services could give you insights, for example, on new usage opportunities or a better understanding of your customer.

In marketing communication you should also think about competitors and complementors as situational and not a fixed element. Some of your competitors could actually complement your message in some dimensions or specific moments. For example, Burger King competes with McDonald's, but symbolically both contribute to a fast food culture.

Beyond Meat takes advantage of a society trend to create a highly successful product.

In IMC we should not just be aware of traditional complementors and competitions, but also to all potential **competitive messages** or **support messages**. These are the messages and discourses that can support or discourage our brand narrative. For example, the 2004 movie "Super Size Me" was a direct attack (competitive message) not just on McDonald's but to most of the fast food business. On the other hand, a new trend can trigger the consumption of your product or support your message even if that trend has nothing to do with your market. For example, an unexpected peak in sales of Mars chocolates was explained because at that time NASA was exploring Mars with important TV coverage. This coverage created a trigger for people purchasing the chocolate (Berger, 2016). A good situational analysis before designing an IMC strategy should consider these elements, as they could provide valuable insight that can be used in the strategy.

So, we have talked about understanding the current brand situation, the different actors involved, and messages affecting your business, but at the center of all of this should be the customer. Insights about **people's needs and wants** are crucial for a good strategic development in marketing communications, but it is also important to understand customer dreams and fears.

With social media we can discover what people are saying about our brand: opinions, complaints, and various sentiments are easily accessible using today's technology. Finally, a good understanding of the customer should include the customer journey and the brand touchpoints that are relevant to them.

Research in IMC

Doing research for IMC is not so very different from any other marketing research. The focus, however, is on understanding how a potential message could be received or where to best reach your customer. Some research involvestestings IMC action or pieces before launching them.

When doing research you have to distinguish first if you are going to use secondary or primary data. **Secondary data** is data that has been collected for other objectives different from your main research objectives. This can be census data or data collected by consulting companies such as Nielsen.

When you don't have the data you need to answer your questions, you will need to perform your own data gathering; this is called **primary data.**

If you are getting the data through primary research then, according to your objectives, you can use **quantitative** or **qualitative** methods. Quantitative methods, such as surveys, have different forms for data collection: face-to-face, online, or via phone. These can also be done by a random sample or using a panel. The selection of the sample size, and quality is extremely important for quantitative research to be accurate.

A large range of methods fall under the label of qualitative research: Interviews, focus groups, observation, netnography, and others (Belk, Fischer & Kozinets, 2012). The sample in qualitative research does not look for statistical representation, however, it should attempt to reach a **redundancy effect**—the point at which the information begins repeating itself and no new information is coming through.

The use of quantitative or qualitative research will depend on your objective. If you want to measure or rank categories, such as consumer preference, you may want to use quantitative methods. On the contrary, if you want to make sense of something in context, such as *why* people preferred something, you will want to use qualitative methods. Most of the time a combination of methods will be more productive and more effective than relying on one method alone.

Social Listening in the New Media

For sure, social media and digital marketing have changed marketing practices and marketing theory. As we discussed previously, these days consumers interact with other consumers and with brands in real time. Brands can also create online brand communities and generate high engagement with consumers. Relevant and fun brand messages can become viral and generate a huge reach for the company. Sometimes users create more brand-related content (both positive and negative) than that generated by the brand itself.

All of the above is great for us as marketers. We will get back to some of these ideas plus more in Chapters 7 and 8. However, something else that is extremely relevant with the new digital media is the capability it gives us to listen to customers as they talk about our brand. From customer reviews on Amazon or Yelp, to Twitter posts complaining about a service, to YouTube videos with user reviews on products or brand communities celebrating a new launch of a movie, all of this gives us a window to the consumers' mind.

Social media allows us to enter consumer conversations and understand how they talk about our brand and other trends.

Some of the benefits of using social media listening are (Minkner, 2019):

- It's in real time: You can get the data as it is happening.
- It's unfiltered: Since you are not asking the customer, the information is less likely to be biased compared to a survey or a focus group.
- It's flexible: You can see changes in trends of opinion.
- It's cost effective: It's not nearly the cost of a formal traditional research.

To access these discussions, we have two different types of data, structured and un-structured data.

As the name suggests, **structured data** is all the data that is already structured for analysis. For example, you can clearly see the number of likes and shares on a Facebook post; the same can be said about Twitter re-tweets.

On the other hand, we have **un-structured data**. In this case the data is more complex to analyze and it has to be structured before you can explore it in its complexity and context. Examples of this can be text in an email message, the content of a Twitter post, or the image shared in an Instagram or Snapshat post.

The use of social listening will depend on your objective and context. Some of the tasks that you can do with the help of different software and platforms are included below:

- Brand mentions can help you identify if users of social media are mentioning your brand and how.
- Identify consumer perception of a product through reviews, such as those on Amazon or Yelp.
- Track sentiments about a brand or message. Some software will allow you to distinguish between positive or negative emotional tones in messages. You could see, for example, positive or negative reactions to your last advertising.
- Identify opinion trends and possible new opportunities or risks related to your brand. This could be done with **topic analysis** using software that can tell you, for example, how people are grouping the topics and which are mentioned the most.
- Track impact of campaigns or explore consumer opinions of competitive products.
- Get marketing leads for your sales team.

- Follow reactions on a crisis scenario and other situations.
- Identify networks and influencers. You can find examples of these in https://nodexlgraphgallery.org/ where social networks were retrieved using a software program called NodeXL (Smith et al., 2010).

Suggested reading to learn more about networks in Twitter conversations: Mapping Twitter Topic Networks: From Polarized Crowds to Community Clusters

---

Voice of the Customer (VOC)

In the marketing field, at some point, you will hear about **Voice of the Customer**, or VOC. VOC is the deep understanding of consumers' (quantitative or qualitative) needs and wants. Different companies use different approaches, to learn what these are. Most use surveys or focus groups, many times in the form of reaction surveys after the use of products or services, but the use of ethnographic methods are also recommended (Goffin, Varnes, van der Hoven & Koners, 2012).

A crucial step to understanding the consumers needs and wants is the Voice of the Customer.

© 13_Phunkod/Shutterstock.com

According to Qualtrics, some recommendations for VOC are (Qualtrics, 2019):

- Use data from different channels and integrate the results.
- All departments should collaborate with the data gathering and with the respective action planning.
- The voice of the employee is important as a representative of the VOC.
- Structure the results and use dashboards to communicate them.
- Understand how the results can improve the ROI.

Consumer Decision-Making Process and the Customer Journey

To better understand consumers and how to reach them, we must understand the consumer decision-making process and how it relates to IMC. Each stage can be influenced from different IMC channels and/or with different messages.

1. **Problem Recognition:** The customer recognizes that they lack something; hunger or thirst will trigger the search for food or drink, for example. A lack of a feature in a product can trigger the want for a new product. Marketing communication can catalyze this stage.

2. **Information Search:** The customer begins a search for a product that can solve his or her needs or wants. The first search is normally internal. This includes brands the consumer already knows about. After that the consumer may engage in a more intense search. IMC can help the customer find information on other good brands that meet their needs.

Understanding the consumer journey can help us decide where to focus the IMC strategy.

© Ihor Bulyhin/Shutterstock.com

3. **Evaluation of Alternatives:** The customer evaluates one or more offers before deciding. IMC can support this process with specific information and comparative advertising at this stage.

4. **Purchase Decision:** Finally, the consumer decides to buy a brand. At this stage IMC can help with sales promotions or with point of sale advertising.

5. **Post-Purchase Evaluation:** After purchase the consumer will evaluate the experience and decide on becoming loyal to the brand, or at least will consider the brand for re-purchase. Direct response marketing, loyalty clubs, and other IMC methods can help in this process.

Some authors have broken these processes into three steps: pre-purchase, purchase, and post purchase. These processes can help us in mapping the **brand touchpoints**.

Mapping Touchpoints

Now that we understand the customer path, we need to think about the specific journey of our consumer. As mentioned in previous chapters, IMC is about giving a consistent message across all the different touchpoints between the brand and the customers. To be able to do this you will need to identify them.

The question here is when and how is the brand reaching the customers? A map or chart should be designed to find the touchpoints, improve them, and/or add new touchpoints.

In the next exercise we show an example of mapping touchpoints according to four types: Brand Owned, Partner Owned, Customer Owned, and or Social/External touchpoints and the three previously mentioned steps of the customer journey. This map can be more specific if needed or vary in different markets.

Exercise: Mapping Touchpoints

Think about your favorite brand and write down all of the interactions or touchpoints that you have with the brand at every stage:

	Pre-Purchase	Purchase	Post-Purchase
Brand or Partner Owned			
Customer Owned			
Social/External			

Customer Brand Decisions

How do customers finally decide what to buy and what not to buy? We already discussed some ideas and the journey for the decision, now we will discuss four different models to explain customer brand decisions.

Some brand decisions fall under what we call an **Evoked Set Model**; this is when the consumer has an evoked or specific set of brands that they will consider choosing from. Let's say that you are looking for tennis shoes; you may consider two or three brands and make the decision to purchase from one of these. These brands are your evoked set.

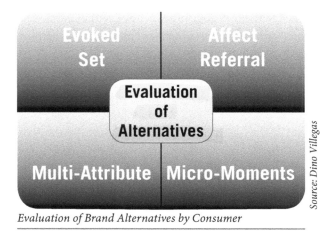

Evaluation of Brand Alternatives by Consumer

In this model we also have two other categories, the **Inept Set**; this is the set of brands that the customer definitively will never buy from. And the **Inert Set**; this is the set of brands that the consumer has no or little information on so cannot actively consider them.

But lets think now about a more complex decision. Let's say that instead of looking for shoes as in the previous case, now you are looking for a doctor for a specific health condition. Would you choose only from a small set of brands that you remember or would you do a more in-depth search comparing attributes and performance records according to you own—conscious or not—ranking of importance? Most likely, it will be the second scenario. This is what we call a **Multi-Attribute Model** of decision.

But sometimes, even in the most complex scenarios, consumption decisions are made strictly based on previous experience. In the search for a doctor example, it's true that most cases would require a Multi-Attribute Model of decision making. You would analyze cost, expertise, insurance coverage, ability to reach the doctor, and more. But if you found yourself in need of the same service again, a probability exists that if you had a good experience you would choose the same provider from before. This emotional connection that leads us to decide on a service because of a good experience in the past is called **Affect Referral**.

With today's technology, some other types of decisions, however, are much faster and not always related to the previously discussed methods. Let's suppose you are walking down the street and you see someone wearing a nice pair of shoes. You can grab your smartphone, take a picture, and look for the shoes online. Immediately, you can buy them or decide not to. This is what Google calls **Micro-Moments** (Ramaswamy, 2015).

Google divides the Micro-Moments category into four types (Google, 2016):

- **I-want-to-know Moments**: Consumer wants to explore something new, not necessary looking to buy right now.
- **I-want-to-go Moments:** Consumer wants to explore a physical shop or store nearby.
- **I-want-to-do Moments:** Consumer is looking for experiences.
- **I-want-to-buy Moments:** Consumer is ready to purchase.

References

Belk, R., Fischer, E., & Kozinets, R. (2012). *Qualitative consumer and marketing research:* Sage.

Berger, J. (2016). *Contagious: Why things catch on:* Simon & Schuster.

Brandenburger, A., & Nalebuff, B. J. (1996). *Co-opetition.* New York: Doubleday.

Goffin, K., Varnes, C. J., van der Hoven, C., & Koners, U. (2012). Beyond the Voice of the Customer: Ethnographic Market Research. *Research-Technology Management, 55*(4), 45–53. doi:10.5437/08956308X5504063

Google. (2016). *The Basics of Micro-Moments.* Retrieved from Think with Google: https://www.thinkwithgoogle.com/marketing-resources/micro-moments/micro-moments-understand-new-consumer-behavior/

Milliken, A. C. N. P. D. C. (2006). Brita: In Search of a Winning Strategy. INSEAD.

Minkner, K. (2019). Why you need social listening in your market research quiver. Retrieved from https://interq-research.com/why-you-need-social-listening-in-your-market-research-quiver/

Qualtrics. (2019). Powerful customer insights. Transformational results. Retrieved from https://www.qualtrics.com/customer-experience/voice-of-customer/

Ramaswamy, S. (2015). How Micro-Moments Are Changing the Rules. Retrieved from https://www.thinkwithgoogle.com/marketing-resources/micro-moments/how-micromoments-are-changing-rules/

Smith, M., Milic-Frayling, N., Shneiderman, B., Mendes Rodrigues, E., Leskovec, J., & Dunne, C. (2010). NodeXL: A free and open network overview, discovery and exploration add-in for Excel 2007/2010.

Tarrant, H. (2019). The bear and bull case for MultiChoice. *Personal Finance Newsletter, 2019*(458), 8–10.

Chapter 3
Segmentation, Targeting, and Positioning

To whom and how we want to be perceived are two of the questions in the STP process. Corona has managed to position itself as a "Mexican beach state of mind" in its target market.

© oneinchpunch/Shutterstock.com

At the heart of any marketing strategy is the Segmentation, Targeting, and Positioning (STP) process. The chapter goes over the STP factors, from a practical perspective, and discusses its importance for an IMC strategy.

Learning Objectives for This Chapter:

- Describe the STP process and its importance for IMC.
- Be able to choose segmentation variables .
- Segment a market according to specific strategy and information.
- Be able to select a targeting segment.
- Be able to write a positioning statement.

STP and the Principles of Marketing

STP decisions are important to any marketing strategy. To understand the why of these decisions, we have to understand the four principles of marketing (Palmatier & Sridhar, 2017):

People are different; they have different tastes and different world views. This is one of the most important elements to be aware of for good marketing.

* **All people differ:** People have different consumption habits, and different wants and needs.
* **People always change:** You are not the same now as you were 10 years ago, and people 10 years younger than you are not the same as you were back then. Society changes and people change.
* **Competition always reacts:** Marketing is a game of multiple actors; it's important to understand the potential moves of the players—the competition.
* **All resources are limited:** Even if you have the biggest marketing budget in the world, your resources are always limited; a good marketing strategy should be a priority.

Because people are different, the same message will not work for everybody. We need to segment people in clusters or groups. Then, because our resources are always limited, we need to choose which of these groups we are going to target. Because the competition will always react, we need to capture a specific position in the mind of the target audience to differentiate ourself and be able to compete. Finally, as our customers change, our marketing strategy should evolve to embrace that change.

But how do we do this STP process? The first element is **segmentation**; this is the identification of various groups that differ in their needs and wants. The second step is **targeting** or choosing one or more segments to focus our marketing efforts on. Finally, the marketer will choose a **positioning** for each of the targets (Kotler & Keller, 2015)

The STP process is extremely important for your marketing strategy as it is going to guide not just your marketing communication but also your marketing mix.

Imagine you're making decisions about marketing a new frozen pizza. For the sake of this example, we'll say that two relevant segments were found: main stream pizza eaters and health conscious consumers. The chart below shows how your decisions would change for each of them:

Example: Decisions for a New Frozen Pizza

Target	Positioning	Product	Price	Place/ Distribution	Promotion
Main Stream Pizza Eater	The most traditional Italian flavors	Italian-themed colors on package	Competitive price with competition	WalMart	TV commercial advertising
Health Conscious Consumers	The only all-natural pizza flavor	Clean package	High-end pricing	Whole Foods	Influencers and health blogs

© Rawpixel.com/Shutterstock.com

A good decision in your STP process is a big part of the potential success of your IMC strategy and execution; a wrong target or position, for example, will put you on the wrong path with all the other decisions you'll need to make about the messages and actions. A well-crafted design in the STP process will be a great starting point for choosing the right message and communication channels.

The Segmentation Process ✳

As we mentioned above, the segmentation process is the process to identify different groups of people with similar needs and wants. This is not just to separate them according to age or location but also recognizing how and why those elements are important for considering them as different segments. It's important to clarify that we don't create segments, we discover them (Palmatier & Sridhar, 2017); because of this, the segmentation variables to consider and the different segments pinpointed must come from well-crafted research.

The basic questions for the segmentation process include: Who are or could be your customers? What have they done or not done in relation to your offer? Why do they make the decisions that they make? (Gupta, 2014). With these answers you will come up with different groups or clusters of people to target. Traditionally, marketing uses five variables to segment consumer markets (even though these variables can sometimes be split into more). The five fundamental variables are discussed below.

Geographic Segmentation

These segments are organized by territory. This could be country, city, region, zip code, urban vs rural, or other divisions. For example, a food company might decide to focus on different geographical segments inside the US because, according to research, they have come to the conclusion that certain states prefer spicy foods and others do not.

Claritas PRIZM

One special form of geodemographic segmentation is the Claritas PRIZM segmentation system; using this sytem you can search for demographics related to specific zip codes.

Go to https://claritas360.claritas.com/mybestsegments/ to learn more about this system.

Demographic Segmentation

Demographic segmentation can be broken apart in many sub-dimensions, such as age, generation, life stage, gender, ethnicity, religion, and more.

For example, a company might focus on different age segments if it has found that the buying behavior for its specific product or service differs between people in the 20–25 age range and those in the 25–35 range. Again, as in geographic segmentation, the importance here will depend on the relevance from the consumer behavior point of view. Do these age groups have different needs and wants related to our offer? If not, then they are not separate segments. To know this, the decision has to be founded in research or be based on actual insights from the consumer.

Sometimes age is important; sometimes life stages are more relevant for segmentation. For example, the following life stages can happen to people at various ages: getting married, going through a divorce, having a baby, and so on.

Psychographic Segmentation

Elements such as the lifestyle of the consumer, the activities that he or she likes, and the personality of the consumer can be important dimensions to consider for grouping them in different segments. For example, we mostly associate energy drinks, like Red Bull or Monster Energy, to extreme sports lovers. However, we could also include people who love to party or late workers in the energy drink segment.

Behavioral Segmentation

In today's marketing era, we look for long-lasting relationships with clients. So, it is no surprise that one possible segmentation variable is how loyal the customer is to our offer. We might also look at the customer's level of involvement, his or her knowledge about the brand, or even the buying stage of the consumer. For example, many companies rank their customers according to levels of loyalty and relevance.

Benefit Segmentation

The benefit that a customer is looking for in a product or offer can be a variable to consider in the segmentation process. For example, a car can be bought as a mode of transportation, as a safe vehicle for the family, or as a status symbol.

Putting It All Together

One of the biggest mistakes you can do when segmenting, is thinking of the previous variables as isolated. I have seen many students and professionals stating that their segmentation will be by age and gender or by psychographics and demographics. Segmentation shouldn't work like that.

As I have mention over this text, segmentation must come from a founded source, be based on good consumer insights, and will usually consist of a mix of all the variables. However, it's true that sometimes you can have only one variable, such as a geographic or age variable, to distinguish your segments; typically, this will be because you've come to the conclusion that this is the most explicative way to separate your potential groups of consumers.

Once you have the different groups in mind, you have to ask yourself if these segments are relevant. The characteristics of useful segments (Clow & Baack, 2018) include the following:

- **Measurable:** Most of the relevant characteristics of the segment can be measured.
- **Substantial:** The segments must be big enough to be interesting; a niche inside a niche that is too specific may not be profitable.
- **Accessible:** Can the brand reach and serve the segment?
- **Differentiable:** Can we really tell the difference between one segment and another? Most importantly, are those differences relevant to why the consumer buys?
- **Actionable:** Can we act on an effective marketing program within this segment?

Selecting the Target Segment ✳

Once you determine a set of potential market segments, you need to select the specific segment or segments among them that you will target. This is important for different reasons. As we mentioned before, in marketing the resources are always limited; so, if you try to target all possible consumers, it likely will not be an efficient way to grow.

Not just that, some of the potential segments can be completely different. For example, let's say you have identified a segment that we are going to call the Traditionalist. You have established that they are a big part of the market and that they don't want to change; they want products that are safe and traditional. On the contrary, another big part of the market is a segment that we will identify as the Innovators. They like products that challenge the status quo and are totally different to established products. If you try to target both of these segments, you will not be able to do it with the same message and/or brand. If you try to be a little bit of both, then most likely you will not be attractive to either of them.

The best way around the previous case is to target the segment that is more attractive for your particular product/context. But, how do we know this? We have three types of questions that you should ask yourself to choose your target or targets.

1. **Questions about the segments:** The first questions you have to ask are about each segment's characteristics. One important element is the size. A segment that is the 25% of the market could be more attractive than a segment of 10% of the market. However, even though the importance of the size is relevant, another element to consider is the **growth rate**. A small segment that is quickly growing can represent a huge opportunity for brands; sometimes better than a big segment that is not growing anymore. Finally, we also have to consider the **profitability** of the segment. For example, luxury or high-income segments, most of the time, are going to be smaller and have a slower growth rate than mainstream segments, but since you can sell your products at a higher price, they may be more profitable than mainstreams.

2. **Questions about the competition:** Now, you already analyzed how attractive a segment is by itself; however, the questioning doesn't stop here. A very attractive segment is probably also a target of multiple brands, so the question about the **intensity of the competition** in the different segments is also very relevant for your success. What **advantages** does your competition have over you in each segment and how many **resources** can they allocate to compete in the segment? These are also relevant questions.

3. **Questions about the brand and the company:** Some segments are going to have a better **fit** with your brand or company, as well as your **mission** and goals. Your attributes and your own **resources** are also elements to consider.

Choosing Your Positioning

Now that you have a target market or different target markets, it is time to choose a place in the mind of those targets. Consider how you want your brand to be perceived by the customers that belong to those segments; this is your positioning.

The concept of positioning was popularize by Ries and Trout in the book *Positioning: The Battle for Your Mind* (Ries & Trout, 1986). Since then the concept has evolved to considering different factors and/or applying different tools. But the main idea is still the same—How can we distinguish ourself from the competition, and occupy a specific space in our target market?

Volvo's positioning traditionally focuses on safety; they reinforce that they are the safest car.

This particular perception about your brand by your customer can be achieved based on different elements, such as a particular **product attribute** (fastest, most durable, etc.) that is unique or at least special to your brand. A **specific applications, price range vs perceived quality**, how the product is **used** by the consumer, or a **symbolic meaning** applicable to your brand.

Another element that we should always consider at the positioning stage is the competition. If what we want is to find a place in the mind of the prospects that is not yet claimed, a competition analysis is must. In this way, one of the useful tools is a positioning statement.

A positioning statement should contain four essential components (Gupta, 2014):

- For whom, for when, for where?
- What value?
- Why and how?
- Relative to whom?

Keep in mind that a positioning statement is not a slogan, but how the brand wants to be perceived. What a company says later on with its slogans and/or claims can be different but should always focus on reinforcing the positioning statement.

Applied Exercise: STP Process

For this exercise choose any brand of your preference.

Brand:			
Segments (four potential segments)			
Segment 1 Description	Segment 2 Description	Segment 3 Description	Segment 4 Description

Target (Choose one of the potential segments):

Explain the reason for choosing that target:

Positioning statement:

References

Clow, K. E., & Baack, D. (2018). *Integrated Advertising, Promotion, and Marketing Communications* (8th ed.).

Gupta, S. (2014). Marketing Reading: Segmentation and Targeting. *Core Curriculum Readings Series.* Boston: Harvard Business Publishing 8219.

Kotler, P. T., & Keller, K. L. (2015). *Marketing Management.* Pearson Education.

Palmatier, R. W., & Sridhar, S. (2017). *Marketing strategy: Based on first principles and data analytics.* Macmillan International Higher Education.

Ries, A., & Trout, J. (1986). *Positioning: The battle for your mind.* McGraw-Hill.

Chapter 4
Brand Creation and Development

We live in a world of brands.

© Bloomicon/Shutterstock.com

We live in a world of symbols; in marketing those symbols are brands. This chapter explores the concept and importance of brands and brand personality, as well as brand elements, such as brand name, logo, and slogans. Finally, the chapter goes into how to build compelling brand stories.

Learning Objectives for This Chapter:

- Discuss the concept and relevance of brand and brand equity.
- Identify the different elements of a brand.
- Distinguish the factors for the successful naming of a brand.
- Distinguish the elements for a quality logo.
- Determine what makes a good slogan.
- Develop a brand personality and the brand voice.
- Design a compelling brand story.

Brand and Brand Equity

Imagine a world without brands!

Now imagine that you are in a supermarket and you have to decide what product to buy in this no-brand world. How would choose? How would you know which one you previously used and liked or didn't like it? How would you recommend a new product to someone?

Brands are useful for us as consumer because they help us differentiate and distinguish the different offers available to us; but how do we define the brand concept? According to the AMA dictionary, a brand is:

How would consumers decide what to buy in a world without brands?

"Name, term, design, symbol, or any other feature that identifies one seller's good or service as distinct from those of other sellers." (marketing-dictionary.org)

But we also have to remember that brands are not just for goods or services; brands are everywhere—from political campaigns, to famous singers, sports drinks, or one of the most important brands for you: your personal brand! This would be your name and its symbolic meaning as well as how others perceive you.

As Laura Oswald would say "A brand is a sign system that engages the consumer in an imaginary/symbolic process of need-fulfillment, differentiates the brand from competitors, and adds measurable value to a product offering" (Oswald & Oswald, 2012, p. 44).

This symbolic value to the product offering also affects the **brand equity**, or the value of the brand as perceived by its customers. As we have mentioned in previous chapters, our IMC strategy is going to have a direct impact on brand equity.

A high brand equity will allow us to charge a premium price vis-à-vis the same product with no brand. Most of the time, the sources of brand equity will consider at least the following (D. A. Aaker, 1992):

* Brand awareness
* Brand loyalty
* Brand perception
* Brand associations

The experience associated with Harley Davidson leads to a high consumer brand equity.

Brand Elements

A brand is made of many different elements that, together, configure the brand identity. Three elements that stand out are the brand name, the brand logo, and the brand slogan (Kohli & Suri, 2002). Some of the characteristics of successful brand elements include being (Farhana, 2012):

* Memorable and distinctive
* Meaningful for the consumer according to the brand category

- Likable and related to the brand style
- Transferable to potential new products and offerings
- Adaptable with the changes in time
- Legally protectable

Brand Elements: The Brand Name

As we discussed earlier, generating brand equity is one of the fundamental purposes of IMC. But how do we do it? In this book we have begun and will continue to discuss it. However, one of the important initial stages in creating brand equity will be the creation of the brand itself, specifically—How do we choose a name that will have better possibilities of growth and be a successful brand?

According to research (Robertson, 1989), these are some of the factors that will help a brand to be more successful:

1. The brand name should be a simple word.
2. The brand name should be a distinctive word.
3. The brand name should be a meaningful word.
4. The brand name should be a verbal or sound associate of the product class.
5. The brand name should elicit a mental image.
6. The brand name should be an emotional word.
7. The brand name should make use of repetitive sounds.
8. The brand name should make use of morphemes.
9. The brand name should make use of phonemes.

This does not mean that a brand has to have every single element from this list but considering these elements will help in the naming process. The element of a meaningful name will repeat itself in the literature as an important component (Klink, 2001, 2003).

Another element to consider when creating a brand name is how explicit the brand should be. The literature describes four categories that go from complete explicate to a name that has no relationship whatsoever with the product (Clow & Baack, 2018):

Bank of America is an example of an overt name.

© Tero Vesalainen/Shutterstock.com

Netflix's implied name has allowed them to grow.

© Kaspars Grinvalds/Shutterstock.com

Amazon's conceptual name comes from the earth's largest river. Also, its logo implies that they currently sell everything from A to Z.

© Sundry Photography/Shutterstock.com

- <u>Overt name:</u> reveals exactly what a company does
- <u>Implied name:</u> contains a mix of words that imply the product category
- <u>Conceptual name:</u> captures the essence of what a company offers
- <u>Iconoclastic name:</u> does not reflect or imply the company offer

When considering a brand name, you have to plan for the potential for brand extension. In this sense an overt name could be too limited. Take, for example, the name Amazon. After considering a diverse range of names, Bezos looked in the dictionary for a word that could represent his vision for the new company as the world largest book store, and he found Amazon listed as the earth's largest river. An easy decision could have been E-Books or even Alexandria (as the greatest library); however, none of those names would have allowed the company to grow to be the biggest store of everything that they are now.

Another good example is Netflix, which has an implied name. Imagine if instead of Netflix they had called themselves something like DVDsbyMail—not only is it not a great name, but it's a very limiting one.

However, an iconoclastic name is not exempt from problems, as it will require more resources and time to effectively position the brand and help consumers make the association with the offering.

A good question for international marketers is when to consider changing the brand name; in an ideal situation, you would use the same brand name everywhere, taking into account the economy of scales and global factors. However, this is not always possible. Sometimes a brand name can be difficult to pronounce in other markets. Take, for example, Kremlyovskaya, the leading vodka brand in Russia. Some authors state that this name may have been a barrier for the brand to grow outside of its native country (A. Ries, 2014).

Brand Elements: Logos

Another important brand element is the logo; this can be one of the most recognizable elements of a brand. Think for a moment of the Nike Swoosh or the Apple logo.

With the emerging trend of smart speakers, such as Alexa or Google assistants, some brands have established what they call a sonic logo or audio logo (Slefo, 2019). A well-known example of this is the famous Intel chimes (O'Reilly, 2016). Logos allow consumers to recognize the brand without reading and sometimes at a distance simply based on colors and design. Some various types of logos are listed below (Morr, 2019):

Monogram Logos: This logo uses only a few letters or initials. The advantage of this type of logos is that they are easy to recognize. However, it must be an established brand to use it successfully. A similar type of logo is the letterforms logo, which contains only one letter; think about the McDonald's M logo (Tailorbrands, 2016).

Wordmark Logos: The use of the brand name with a specific typography as the logo. The most famous of these types of logos is Coca-Cola

Brand Marks: An icon or symbol-based logo that has a strong connection with the brand, like the apple from Apple or the bird for Twitter.

Abstract Logo Marks: Similar to brand marks, abstract logos are based on images that represent the brand but are completely abstract. These allow the brand to be truly unique but can be more difficult to position.

Mascots: Some brands choose to represent themselves with a mascot, like KFC's Colonel or the gecko from Geico. Mascots can add personality to a brand but sometimes they can outgrow the brand or vice versa. Also, if they are more complex ,they could be difficult to transfer between media.

Combination Logo: A combination of a symbol or a mascot with a wordmark, these types of logos are useful to position a new brand. Sometimes after they are well-known, brands can use just the symbol or mascot.

Emblem: A more traditional approach that mixes a symbol with text inside, these types of logos look like a seal or a badge. Think about the Harley-Davidson or Starbucks logo.

This Twitter logo is an example of a brand mark.

© rvlsoft/Shutterstock.com

The Pepsi logo is an example of an abstract logo mark.

© PhotoTodos/Shutterstock.com

Geico mascot.

© Casimiro PT/Shutterstock.com

Most of the time, Burger King uses a combination logo.

© 8th creator/Shutterstock.com

Starbucks use an emblem as their logo.

© urbanbuzz/Shutterstock.com

HBO is an example of a monogram logo.

© Casimiro PT/Shutterstock.com

Coca-Cola is one of the most recognizable wordmark logos.

© phloxii/Shutterstock.com

Other factors to consider when thinking about a brand logo is the typography to use and the colors. Both of these have symbolic implications. Colors, for example, have specific meanings (Adams, Morioka & Stone, 2004); red can mean passion; yellow, joy; blue, calm, etc.

When creating a logo, the marketer should be careful to use professional services. Some companies try to skip the cost of professional services and, most of the time, this results in poor quality logos. It's important to make sure your logo is adjustable based on various mediums. You have to consider how the logo will look on a screen as well as in print, How will it look like in a black and white platform? Will the colors change between platforms? All of these are important issues to consider.

Brand Elements: Slogans

Other important brand elements are slogans and taglines; although these words are sometimes used synonymously, they do have a slightly different meaning. According to Laura Ries, slogans should stick to the brand and taglines can be mobile between campaigns (L. Ries, 2015).

Slogans should not be confused with the positioning statement. As with the other two brand elements, slogans should translate the positioning statement to the consum-

The Nike "Just Do It" slogan is one of the most recognizable brand battle cries.

© pio3/Shutterstock.com

ers. Also, the marketer should be very conscious of the objective that a specific slogan has. A good slogan should reinforce the positioning, be liked by the consumer, or be easy to recall. Some of the factors that contribute to likability of brand slogan are listed below (Dass, Kumar, Kohli, Kumar, & Thomas, 2014):

- Clarity in the slogan
- Emphasis of benefits
- Creativity in the slogan

- Appropriate and related to the product
- Using rhymes

Developing a Brand: Brand Personality and the Brand Voice

To develop strong brands, we should begin with some key questions:

- What are the current levels of brand awareness and brand positioning?
- What do you want to achieve with the brand?
- What are the brand's strengths and weaknesses?
- What are the brand's opportunities and threats?
- What are your competitive advantages and resources?

The answers to these questions will give you an important starting point for your brand. However, to develop strong brands, you must develop a strong **brand personality**. But what is brand personality? It is assigning human characteristics or traits to a brand (J. L. Aaker, 1997). The process of humanizing brands is also known as **anthropomorphization** (Aggarwal & McGill, 2012; Portal, Abratt & Bendixen, 2018).

To understand brand persona you need to ask yourself how you would describe the brand as a person. Would it be agile or conservative; would it be old and experienced or young and bold? Would it more likely be a woman or a man?

The understanding of the brand persona will allow you to understand how your brand should behave. For example, if you are using social media, you'll want to determine if this brand will be funny or serious, risky or conservative.

Traditionally in marketing we have five macro dimensions of brand personality that most brands can choose from:

- Sincerity
- Excitement
- Competence
- Sophistication
- Ruggedness

The brand personality can be represented also in the brand voice or tone of voice (Barcelos, Dantas & Sénécal, 2018); this is a communication or linguistic style that the brand will use in its different applications. In other words, this is the way the brand talks. We need to understand that the style is not necessarily the content that the brand will talk about but how it will be said. You know this from a human-to-human perspective; some people sound nicer than others, or more formal or informal, or use more personal pronouns. We all have our own style of speaking.

Wendy's has a very recognizable brand voice on Twitter.

© rafapress/Shutterstock.com

For example, some research has proved that in the case of more traditional brands ,an informal tone is not always the best alternative (Gretry, Horváth, Belei & van Riel, 2017). We also know that changes between the use of "I" or "we" can have an effect on consumers attitudes toward brands (Sela, Wheeler & Sarial-Abi, 2012).

One of the most important things about brand voice is consistency over time. This is particularly difficult in social media where you have more than one person posting in name of the brand.

The Power of Brand Stories

Branding has always been about creating and managing signature stories that represent brand personas. Today, those stories have to compete in real time with thousands of other stories generated by users around the world, and companies have to take extra steps to be able to distinguish themselves. You need to be able to tell a story, a narrative, with your brand.

It has been proven that stories work better than facts in the mind (D. Aaker, 2018). It is easy for us to **remember** stories, and we can often see ourselves in the shoes of the protagonist. This activates what we call the mirror neurons (Manney, 2008); because of this, stories are also more persuasive.

Studies on rumor and word of mouth have proven that stories also have a higher probability of **becoming viral** over mere facts.

According to David Aaker (D. Aaker, 2018), good signature brand stories have to have at least these four characteristics:

1. Intriguing: The story awakens the curiosity of the customer; people want to know where the story is going and what's next!
2. Authentic: The story sounds authentic inside the world being created.
3. Involving: The story involves the user.
4. Strategic Message: The story should not lose sight of the fact that it is meant to support a marketing purpose.

Brand stories can consist of one singular **standalone story**, such as the story of the founder or the company. We have heard many times how Steve Jobs or Bill Gates created their companies in their respective garages, for example. However, one story is not always possible or desirable. Sometimes you want to have many stories that taken together can generate a **brand narrative**. One good option for this multiple story telling is to have a **brand portfolio** where you have multiple stories available that can be told in different circumstances.

Steve Jobs was a master in storytelling; this always translated well to Apple marketing.

© Anton_Ivanov/Shutterstock.com

One element that many stories have in common is a **hero**. A literature professor named Joseph John Campbell, after studying many myths over human history, realized that all these heroes had the same structure (Campbell, 1994). This is what he called the Hero's Journey. The hero's journey has 17 steps. Other authors have presented some modifications to some of these steps; however, all of them can be summarized in three stages:

1. **The Departure:** The hero, receives a call to adventure that he will refuse at first; a supernatural mentor will help him accept the adventure.
2. **Initiation:** The hero will go over a series of tests, including specific temptations; the hero will achieve his or her quest.
3. **Return:** The hero will begin the journey back and will return with the " elixir" or answer.

Movies such as Iron Man, The Matrix, The Hunger Games, and many others have used the journey of the hero to develop their characters. Brands can do the same.

Suggested Video: The HERO'S JOURNEY - Joseph Campbell

In marketing the hero doesn't always have to be the brand. For example, in some brands, the customer is the hero and the brand is just the path for the hero. For a local provider or the local community, you can find heroes for your brand story in:

- The founder
- A transformational CEO
- An employee
- A supplier
- The customer
- The program
- Business transformation
- The product or the offering

Brand Portfolio and Brand Extension

So far, we have discussed brands as one single element for one specific offering; however, this is more complex in most companies today. The majority of large corporations today will have **brand portfolios**; this is a group of brands under one company. For example, P&G has multiple brands, such as Ariel, Charmin, Always, and more. A different example is Apple. They use the Apple name on all their products, adding a sub-brand to each model; this is what we call a **branded house**.

In 2002, Porsche took a huge risk incorporating the first SUV in its history. The SUV was far from everything that Porsche meant up until this point; however, the play worked and opened up new markets for the brand.

One of the big discussions in the literature and in company decision rooms is about **brand extensions**. This is the idea of using the brand elements in a new line of products. Normally, this introduces the risk of diluting the brand, but if implemented successfully, it can open great opportunities for the company. The new product line will benefit from the existing positive associations of the brand; however, if the new product line is not symbolically close to the original line of products, the effect may not be positive at all. Worse, negative associations of the new product line can negatively affect the original brand.

Decisions on brand extension have to be carefully measured, assessing the strength of the brand equity and its elasticity, considering also how close the new product line is to existing products, and the potential benefits and risks of the decision.

Application Exercise

Think about a brand that you use daily and answer the questions.

Brand:
Brand Personality:
What's your expert opinion on the brand name?
What's your expert opinion on the brand logo?
What's your expert opinion on the brand slogan?

References

Aaker, D. (2018). *Creating Signature Stories: Strategic Messaging That Energizes, Persuades, and Inspires.* New York: Morgan James.

Aaker, D. A. (1992). The Value of Brand Equity. *Journal of Business Strategy, 13*(4), 27–32. doi:10.1108/eb039503

Aaker, J. L. (1997). Dimensions of brand personality. *Journal of Marketing Research, 34*(3), 347–356.

Adams, S., Morioka, N., & Stone., T. (2004). *Logo design workbook:* Rockport.

Aggarwal, P., & McGill, A. L. (2012). When Brands Seem Human, Do Humans Act Like Brands? Automatic Behavioral Priming Effects of Brand Anthropomorphism. *Journal of Consumer Research, 39*(2), 307–323. doi:10.1086/662614

Barcelos, R. H., Dantas, D. C., & Sénécal, S. (2018). Watch Your Tone: How a Brand's Tone of Voice on Social Media Influences Consumer Responses. *Journal of Interactive Marketing, 41*, 60–80.

Campbell, J. (2008). The hero with a thousand faces. California: New World Library.

Clow, K., & Baack, D. (2018). *Integrated Advertising, Promotion, and Marketing Communications* (8 ed.).

Dass, M., Kumar, P., Kohli, C., Kumar, P., & Thomas, S. (2014). A study of the antecedents of slogan liking. *Journal of Business Research, 67*(12). https://doi.org/10.1016/j.jbusres.2014.05.004

Farhana, M. (2012). Brand elements lead to brand equity: Differentiate or die. *Information management and business Review, 4*(4), 223–233.

Gretry, A., Horváth, C., Belei, N., & van Riel, A. C. (2017). "Don't pretend to be my friend!" When an informal brand communication style backfires on social media. *Journal of Business Research, 74*, 77–89.

Klink, R. R. (2001). Creating Meaningful New Brand Names: A Study of Semantics and Sound Symbolism. *Journal of Marketing Theory and Practice, 9*(2), 27–34. doi:10.1080/10696679.2001.11501889

Klink, R. R. (2003). Creating Meaningful Brands: The Relationship Between Brand Name and Brand Mark. *Marketing Letters, 14*(3), 143–157. doi:10.1023/a:1027476132607

Kohli, C., & Suri, R. (2002). Creating effective logos: Insights from theory and practice. *Business Horizons, 3*(45), 58–64.

Manney, P. (2008). Empathy in the Time of Technology: How Storytelling is the Key to Empathy. *Journal of Evolution & Technology, 19*(1).

marketing-dictionary.org. (Ed.).

Morr, K. (2019). The 7 types of logos (and how to use them). Retrieved from https://99designs.com/blog/tips/types-of-logos/

O'Reilly, L. (2016). The 10 most effective brand jingles—From the Intel chimes to 'I'm Lovin' it'. Retrieved from https://www.businessinsider.com/the-10-most-recognizable-brand-audio-logos-2016-11

Oswald, L. R., & Oswald, L. (2012). *Marketing semiotics: Signs, strategies, and brand value:* Oxford University Press.

Portal, S., Abratt, R., & Bendixen, M. (2018). Building a human brand: Brand anthropomorphism unravelled. *Business Horizons, 61*(3), 367–374.

Ries, A. (2014). Biggest change in marketing in last 50 years might get lost in translation. Retrieved from https://adage.com/article/al-ries/biggest-change-marketing-lost-translation/296067

Ries, L. (2015). Slogans vs. Taglines: What is your brand's Battlecry? Retrieved from https://adage.com/article/cmo-strategy/slogans-taglines-brand-s-battlecry/301217

Robertson, K. (1989). Strategically desirable brand name characteristics. *Journal of Consumer Marketing, 6*(4), 61–71.

Sela, A., Wheeler, S. C., & Sarial-Abi, G. (2012). We are not the same as you and I: Causal effects of minor language variations on consumers' attitudes toward brands. *Journal of Consumer Research, 39*(3), 644–661.

Slefo, G. (2019). PANDORA UNVEILS ITS FIRST SONIC LOGO. Retrieved from https://adage.com/creativity/work/pandora-sonic-logo/1729321

Tailorbrands. (2016). The 9 Types of Logos & How to Use Them. Retrieved from https://www.tailorbrands.com/logo-maker/types-of-logos

Chapter 5
IMC Mix Planning

With so many media choices, IMC planning is critical to campaign success.

© Oliver Le Moal/Shutterstock.com

Good IMC planning depends, in part, on well-crafted objectives and metrics. The first part of this chapter goes over these important decisions. The second part of the chapter discusses how to set a budget for IMC. Finally, the chapter ends with going over the different media choices and the criteria to select them.

Learning Objectives for This Chapter:

- Recognize the importance of objective setting and metrics.
- Formulate objectives for an IMC campaign.
- Design a set of metrics for an IMC campaign.
- Plan a budget for an IMC campaign.

- Differentiate between own, paid, and earned media.
- Distinguish the major marketing communication media categories.
- Choose media and channels according to strategic criteria.

Setting Your Objectives

IMC, as any other discipline, is about knowing what you want to achieve. In other words, you have to know where you are going to be able to arrive there.

Our IMC strategy will depend on our marketing strategy, which depends on the business and corporate strategy. So, the question for IMC setting is: How can we contribute to those objectives?

For this, we need to break down the business and marketing objectives into more specific areas. For example, if we need more sales the question will be: Where will those sales come from. For example, do we need more leads? Or maybe just better quality leads? Or do we need to create a new consumption pattern? Or perhaps the sales objective should be attracting a new target market. Whatever the answer, the next question is how media and message can contribute to the achievement of those goals. After having a clear

The IMC strategy of the last Avengers movie was not only to bring people to the movie theaters, but also to be in line with the objectives of Marvel Studios (business unit) and those of Walt Disney Company (corporate).

understanding of the IMC contribution, we will need to quantify how the achievement of those goals will be measured. Finally, socialization with the entire company team is important (Young, 2014).

One mistake that we often see when setting IMC goals is the setting of low-level goal instead of high-level goals. This is especially true with social media where many brands will set up goals as a number of likes per month or a number of shares. These are performance indicators, and even though that may be important, most of the time, they are not the goal itself but just a metrics to reach the goal.

Anthony Young (Young, 2014) describes this as outputs and not outcomes. The relevant question here is: Is this really the objective that we are trying to achieve? Any other metric that we can consider should support those goals.

A good and easy example, unrelated to IMC, that we can think of is when you are trying to lose weight. In this case, you typically measure the number of calories that you are consuming and the number of calories you are expending; however, those metrics, even though they are fundamental, are not the main objective.

Some examples of IMC program goals are:

- Create or increase awareness.
- Increase consumer understanding about the brand.
- Increase brand appeal to target X.
- Build trust for target x.
- Elicit emotions about the brand.
- Inspire action.
- Increase sales.
- Build loyalty.

Setting Your Metrics

As we mentioned before, setting objectives is just a first step. The need to measure the progression on these objectives is equally or more important. Your metrics have to be in direct relationship with your goal.

Some objectives can be measured directly as, for example, number of sales or conversion rates. However, not all objectives can be measured directly and may require other tools or indirect methods to do this, such as conducting surveys.

Your metrics have to be in direct sight of your objectives.

Also, when considering metrics and objectives, you should consider result-oriented and **process-oriented metrics** so you can see how are you doing and determine room for improvement.

An example of a result-oriented metric is the number of sales made; examples of process- oriented metrics can be number of people reached or number of leads obtained.

Some of the most used IMC metrics are:

- **Average acquisition cost:** The average cost to acquire a new client.
- **Brand awareness:** Percentage of consumers who recognize a specific brand. (marketing-dictionary.org)
- **Brand knowledge:** Consumers' level of knowledge about the brand/product.
- **CLV:** Customer Lifetime Value or average monetary value of customers according to the present value of the projected cash flows from all consumer interaction. (marketing-dictionary.org)
- **Engagement:** Different authors and different companies use the engagement concept in various ways; however, most of the time the concept will refer to interactions between brands and consumer.
- **Market share:** Percentage of the market for a specific brand. (marketing-dictionary.org)
- **Net promoter score:** A specific measure to understand a customer's willingness to recommend a product.
- **Retention rates:** Ratio of the number of customer retained. (marketing-dictionary.org)
- **RMI:** Return on Marketing Investment is the contribution to the profits by marketing programs. (marketing-dictionary.org)
- **Abandonment rate:** Ratio of number of shopping carts ready to buy that didn't complete the process. (marketing-dictionary.org)
- **Click-through rate:** Ratio of the number of customers that click on a link.
- **Cost per click:** The average cost per click normally used for online advertising.
- **CPM:** Cost per Thousand (or Mille) the cost to reach a thousand people as a measure to standardize the cost of media; this also can be measured as Cost per Contact.
- **Frequency:** Average of number of times that a brand will reach an audience.
- **GRP:** Gross Rating Points are calculated as a percent of the target market reached multiplied by the exposure frequency.
- **Ratings:** Number of TVs on a specific show divided by the number of TVs in the market.

- **Reach:** Number of people reached with an ad.
- **Redemption rates:** Used mostly for coupons and rebates, it is the rate of the number of people that use the sales promotion.
- **Sales:** Number of sales.
- **Share of voice:** Share of exposure a brand gets vs. the competition.
- **Share of customer:** The share that the company has of a customer buying its products vs. buying other brands.

Don't think of this list as a compressive one, as IMC has many more metrics that we could use. We will go over some of them in later chapters of this book, as they fit with the different media platforms that we will study.

Application Exercise

Imagine you are the Marketing Director of a golf club and you are preparing a campaign for next year. Following the example provided, choose three more objectives, metrics, and targets.

Objective	Metrics	Target
New members	Members growth rate	10% of growth rate at the end of next year

Setting the Budget

Your objectives and strategy will be influenced by what is possible and how much money you are budgeting to invest in media and IMC production. The decision on how much to invest is a delicate one and needs to be done with much thought. In small companies this decision is often based on what they can afford; however, as you can image, this is not the best approach. Other ways to determine the budget are (Clow & Baack, 2018):

- A percentage of past year sales
- Payout planning from future forecasted income
- A meet-the-competition approach

These three methods have many shortcomings. For example, basing your budget on past sales can limit your future growth; sometimes you want to go anti-cyclical with your sales and your promotion efforts. The same is true for projected future income. A meet-the-competition approach is no better, as it will let the competition dictate your strategy.

A much better approach would be what the literature calls **Objectives and Task** (Clow & Baack, 2018). This includes a breakdown of your objectives, assigning value to them, and planning the tasks necessary to reach them.

Defining your budget is just the first step of the budgeting process. The second part is deciding how that budget is going to be divided across the year. Typically, we use three different strategies for this:

Pulsating schedule: Advertising throughout the entire year with bursts of additional spending at select times, such as during holidays.

Flighting schedule: Allocates the budget only during peak times, with no other times scheduled during the year.

Continuous schedule: Divides the budget equally throughout the entire year.

Planning the IMC Mix: Understanding the Media

So, we have talked about the brand and the message; however, how we deliver that message is extremely important as well. To determine this, we need to understand the arsenal of channels of communications that we have at our disposal. One way that we can differentiate the types of media is with the concept of **Own, Paid,** or **Earned Media** (Stephen & Galak, 2012):

Own Media: This is the media that the brand owns; examples of own media include company brochures, TV channels, retail in-store visual merchandising, company websites, company blogs, and social media accounts of the brand, to name a few.

Paid Media: This is the media that the brand pays for, including traditional advertising, online advertising, sponsorships, and social media advertising among others.

Earned Media: This includes brand touchpoints not generated directly by the brand, but by other agents, such as journalists or consumers. Examples include public relations, consumer reviews, word of mouth recommendations, social media mentions, and more.

Other than these three major categories, we can name new IMC alternatives that can be a mix of these. For example, some **Influencer** campaigns can be a blend of earned and paid media; advertising by paying for distributing a company's own content can be considered a mix between paid and own media; and SEO efforts that attract users to the brand webpage is a mix between earned and own media (Kumar, 2016).

Red-Bull has its own TV channel.

© dennizn/Shutterstock.com

Yahoo uses paid media to advertise in Times Square.

© Anton_Ivanov/Shutterstock.com

Customer reviews have changed the way businesses interact with customers and is one of the most relevant avenues in earned media today.

© Black Salmon/Shutterstock.com

Many authors group the media channels in different ways. For the purpose of this book we are clustering these in five categories, according to the effect on the brand, as can be seen in the table below:

Media Category	Characteristics	Media Channel Examples
Advertising the Brand	Mostly massive but have to decide on the reach vs. frequency dilemma to balance the budget, control of the message, paid media	TV, radio, uut-of-home advertising, print media
The Brand in the Digital Space	Can be paid, own, or earned; highly interactive; some channels lack message control. High capability to measure.	Internet advertising, blogs, websites, and mobile marketing
The Social Brand	A branch of digital, focus on social media. High measurement, can be massive and customizable.	Social media ads, social media management, real time marketing, viral marketing, influencers, brand communities
The Brand in the Public	Mostly earned, as in public relations where the message is difficult to control, can be as massive as advertising. Also events and other channels are paid media and have better control of the message but normally are more targeted.	Press coverage, press releases, events, sponsorships, cause marketing
Selling the Brand	Efforts focus on transforming the brand equity in sales or in generating specific behaviors from the client.	Personal selling, direct response marketing, sales promotions

Choosing the IMC Mix

When deciding what media to use, it is important to do it with a strategic vision and be consistent between each touchpoint; every message in every channel should conduct the campaign to a specific previously defined objective. Some of the criteria when choosing the IMC channels are listed below (Batra & Keller, 2016):

- **Coverage:** How much of the target market can we reach with the IMC mix that we are choosing? How can we look for media that can reach portions of the target market not reached by others channels?
- **Cost:** The different criteria should be evaluated against the cost. What are some more financially effective ways to reach our goals?
- **Contribution:** How does each of the media in the IMX mix create the desired response in the consumer? Are they building awareness? Moving to buy? Or affecting any other stage in the consumer journey?
- **Commonality:** The mix of some media can reinforce the associations of other media by sharing the same meaning in the messages.
- **Complementary:** Some mixes of media can not only act together but also reinforce the message of the other media
- **Cross-Effects:** Can the client be encouraged to interact between different media channels? For example, you might have a TV ad asking the audience to go on Facebook to do something specific or perhaps finish watching the ad on YouTube.
- **Conformability:** The ability of the mix to work across targets and/or througout the consumer journey.

Application Exercise

Choose any campaign you have seen this month and answer:

Brand/Campaign:
What media is the campaign using (name at least three)?
Reasons (Why do you think this campaign chose those forms of media? Is there any interaction or cross-effect between them?):

References

Batra, R., & Keller, K. L. (2016). Integrating marketing communications: New findings, new lessons, and new ideas. *Journal of Marketing, 80*(6), 122–145.

Clow, K., & Baack, D. (2018). *Integrated Advertising, Promotion, and Marketing Communications* (8 ed.).

Kumar, S. (2016). Balancing Paid, Owned, and Earned Media to Maximize Content Reach. Retrieved from https://insights.newscred.com/balancing-paid-owned-and-earned-media-to-maximize-content-reach/

marketing-dictionary.org. (Ed.).

Stephen, A. T., & Galak, J. (2012). The Effects of Traditional and Social Earned Media on Sales: A Study of a Microlending Marketplace. *Journal of Marketing Research, 49*(5), 624–639. doi:10.1509/jmr.09.0401

Young, A. (2014). *Strategy: Integrated Communications Planning in the Digital Era:* Springer.

Chapter 6
Advertising the Brand

It is true that with the new media, families don't spend as much time watching traditional TV channels as before. However, TV, radio, out-of-home, and print media are all still relevant today.

© Andrey_Popov/Shutterstock.com

This chapter discusses the factors for the successful use of traditional media. First, we cover the three stages of message development: strategy, appeal, and framework. Then, we go over the four categories of traditional media: TV, radio, out-of -home (outdoor) advertising, and print media. Finally, we discuss some of the elements to consider for choosing the right advertising agency.

Learning Objectives for This Chapter:

- Recognize the importance of advertising.
- Discuss the relevance and the role of creativity in advertising.
- Distinguish the three factors of an advertising message.
- Develop an advertising message.

- Differentiate between reach and frequency.
- Differentiate and decide on the best traditional media according to specific objectives.
- Identify relevant factors for choosing an advertising agency.

The Importance of Advertising

Many times, when we talk about marketing, people who are not familiar with the field think of either just advertising and/or sales. As we have discussed in earlier chapters, marketing is not only those things. Advertising is, however, an important part of the portfolio of tools in the marketing communication arsenal.

What we now refer to as traditional advertising—TV, newspapers, out-of-home (outdoor), radio, and magazines—may not be as popular (especially among young people) as they used to be; however, they are still important options in your IMC strategy.

As we discussed in previous chapters, today's consumer attention is often spread out among different media at the same time. Because of this we cannot think of any media—traditional, digital, or otherwise—as isolated. For example, we need to remember that people can be watching TV at the same time that they are looking at their mobile phone screen. New technology today allows us to somehow account for this.

Creativity in Advertising

An important but sometimes controversial concept in advertising is creativity. Agencies, on one hand, search for the spark of creativity as much as they can; they value creativity and sometimes work toward winning international creativity contests. Clients (brands), on the other hand, are not always equally enthusiastic about creativity; they demand affectivity and strategic thinking. These two positions, however, shouldn't be in opposition. Creativity does have an important place not only in advertising but also in marketing. However, creativity just for the sake of creativity is not what you want. Creativity should always serve the objectives and strategy.

Creativity in advertising can be understood in five dimensions (Reinartz & Saffert, 2013):

1. **Originality:** Something new and original can surprise the audience and grab their attention; however, much of advertising is just more of the same.

© IStock Studio/Shutterstock.com

In 2019 the CEO of Mercedes Benz resigned after 49 years. The same day of the announcement, BMW responded with a very original move. They created a salute video saying that he was finally free to choose a BMW.

Recommended Video: CEO of Mercedes resigned after 49 years. BMW released this ad the moment it was announced.

2. **Flexibility:** The product is shown in a range of different uses or ideas.

3. **Elaboration:** This dimension is about using simple ideas in a different way, showing more details.

4. **Synthesis:** Connecting or blending unrelated objects in the mind of the consumer to create a new image.

5. **Artistic value:** The use of language, images, or sounds in an artistic or aesthetically pleasing form.

Creativity is an important part of advertising. Different methods can help to deliver creative ideas.

Suggested Reading: 9 Creative Techniques for You and Your Team

Creating the Advertising Message

The creation and development of the advertising message has to be a progressive translation of your research, goals, and, of course, your targeting and positioning.

For example, a campaign that is looking to create awareness will look completely different from one that wants to educate the consumer or create brand loyalty. Of course, a different target will change our message appeal and the message itself will be defined by the positioning statement.

Also, the message has to be carefully crafted and tested for how the consumer might respond to it. Some advertising messages have had problems with getting a completely opposite reaction from the one they were looking for.

Not only is the consumer reaction important in every marketing move, but the potential competition response is also important. When we design a message, what we are doing is framing a concept in the mind of our prospects; the competition can try to frame the same message to their advantage or dilute our messaging.

To create the advertising message there are three steps that we need to consider: the message strategy, the election of the message appeals, and the executional framework of the message (Clow & Baack, 2018).

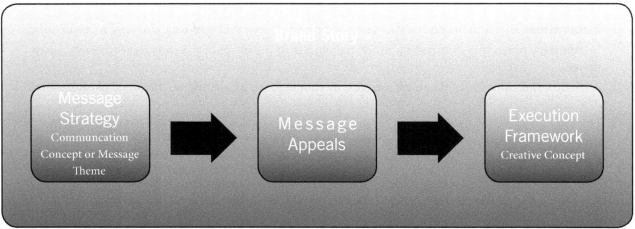

Three steps to design the advertising message

Source: Dino Villegas

The Message Strategy

So, the first step to designing the advertising message is to select the strategy. In general, we can find three different strategies to work on (Clow & Baack, 2018): Cognitive Message Strategy, Affective Message Strategy, and Conative Message Strategy. Each of these strategies will be more appropriate in different stages of the consumer journey. For example, a Cognitive Strategy is usually used in the awareness or research stages; the Affective Strategy, on the other hand, would be more appropriate for creating loyalty among current customers; while a Conative Strategy seeks to move the consumer to a specific action.

A Cognitive Strategy focuses the message on a specific attribute of the offering.. It is important to note that, as we are going to discuss later, even if it is a Cognitive Strategy, this does not mean that the appeal or execution will be rational; it only means that the message will be focused on a specific attribute or consumer benefit. The Cognitive Strategy can be divided into five different sub-strategies:

- **Generic:** When you are the leader of a market, you may want to advertise an attribute of the product category. In cases like this, the brand will not advertise superiority to the competition, but relies on the fact that, for many users, their brand is synonymous with the category.

- **Preemptive:** The use of an advantage or attribute before the competition focuses on it, to lock the position in the mind of the consumers.

- **Unique selling proposition:** Maybe the attribute or advantage cannot be easily copied and you have proven it; in this case we use USP.

Verizon uses a Cognitive Strategy as they promote a better network. This has sometimes led to a message battle with the competition and to comparative advertising.

- **Hyperbole:** The utilization of an attribute in a fictional, exaggerated way, such as "Red Bull gives you wings."

- **Comparative:** The direct comparison of the attributes with a competitive brand.

An **Affective Strategy** instead will focus the message on the connection of the brand with the consumer and/or the experiences it can generate. Keep in mind that this is the strategy and the main theme and not the tone of the message. Some emotional messages can be cognitive as they try to focus on a specific attribute.

Finally, a **Conative Strategy** will focus the message on a call for action. Examples of this are "Call Now" campaigns or claims such as "buy before it's gone.

Message Appeals

After the strategy the next consideration is for the appeal of the message. If the strategy was "what" to say, the appeal is the general how to say it. Also, keep in mind that advertising messages can have more than one appeal. Some of the most well-known appeals are:

Humor: Appealing to humor in advertising has proven to be very effective, some considerations to have when appealing to humor are noted below.

- Humor can enhance the memorability and attitude toward advertising (Chung & Zhao, 2003).
- Humor can attract the attention of consumers (Weinberger & Gulas, 1992).
- Some products can have a better effect using humor than others (IDEM).
- Humor must be used carefully and ethically to not stereotype a group of people.
- Humor can "eat" the brand, generating the effect of people remembering the "joke" but not the brand.

Fear: Some brands use fear as the main message appeal. Services like insurance will be obvious choices for this type of appeal. As with humor, the fear appeal can be effective but also has some issues to consider. The first consideration is the range of fear; too much and people will mentally—or physically, such as changing the channel—block the message. Too little and it will not have an effect at all. A second consideration is the perception of the probability of occurrence. If you cannot show or persuade people that this could happened to them, the fear appeal will be diluted.

The Coca-Cola polar bears campaign is focused on the relationship of the brand with the consumers and not on a specific attribute of the product.

Advertising of sales promotions such as this one are considered Conative; the focus is on moving to the sale.

"Eat mor Chikin" say the Chick-fil-A cows, using a humorous way to deliver the message.

Music: Music can work very well in TV and radio advertising, especially in combination with other appeals. A research by Nielsen done in 2015 showed those TV commercials that used some type of music performed better than non–music–based commercials in four specific dimensions: creativity, empathy, emotive power, and information power (Nielsen, 2015).

Music in advertising can have many forms. For example, some advertising uses popular music (Allan, 2006), while others create a specific jingle to communicate the brand slogan (Yalch, 1991). Sometimes music will just be used in the background of the advertising (Kellaris & Cox, 1989).

Emotions: Another alternative is to appeal directly to the emotions. This type of appeal is not necessarily just for Affective Strategies but can also be used in Cognitive ones. For example, a diaper's brand can focus its message on a particular attribute (Cognitive), such as the dry capabilities of the diaper; however, to communicate the message, they may want to appeal to the emotional attachment of the parents with their children's well-being.

Sensuality and/or Sex: Sex appeal in advertising has a very extensive range that can go from just a hint of sensuality to a more explicit symbol of a sex act. Note that sex appeal advertising used to be very common; however, it looks like its popularity is declining. One interesting example is the diminished use of sex appeal advertising in the latest Super Bowl commercials (Taylor, 2019).This type of change can stem from marketers understanding that today's society is more sensitive to the objectification of women and because of movements like #MeToo.

Another factor to consider is that research has shown that even though sex appeal can enhance the memorability and recall of an ad, it will not necessarily translate to brand recall or, even more important, result in sales conversions (Wirtz, Sparks & Zimbres, 2018). This, however, may be different for sex-=related products, such as the condom (Chiang, Chan & Milan, 2018). Also, in advertising for some beauty products, we can still see some sensual appeal.

Rationality: Some advertising is strictly rational and will support an argument with statistics, testimonies, or other similar tools.

Scarcity: This type of appeal shows that the need for action is now because the offer will expire soon; this is mostly used with a Conative Strategy.

Executional Framework

After choosing the strategy and appeal, the next question relates to the specifics of the how. The executional framework will explain how the story in the advertising will be told. Some possible frameworks include:

- **Animation:** The use of animation to express the message
- **Slice-of-life:** A real life moment, where the protagonist has a day-to-day problem solved by the brand
- **Storytelling:** A short story where the brand or the consumer is the hero or the protagonist
- **Testimonial:** A testimony of a current user or person connected with the brand
- **Authoritative:** An authority testimony of the quality of the offering
- **Demonstration:** A simple demonstration to educate on the use of the brand
- **Fantasy:** The creation of a fantasy world related to the brand
- **Informative:** Direct information about the brand

Many detergent advertisers uses slice-of-life stories; in a normal day-to-day scenario, someone is going to have an unexpected accident that will lead to a stain, and the detergent will solve the problem.

Application Exercises

In www.imcstrategy.com, go to suggested material and look for "CANNES LIONS 2018 WINNERS" after watching some of the videos, choose the one that you like the most and answer the following:

Brand and Campaign:
Objective
Message Strategy
Message Appeal

Traditional Media

Together with the advertising message, another task in traditional advertising is the decision on the media.

One element that is important to consider in traditional media is the tension between reach and frequency. Reach is the average number of times that your ad will impact your target, and frequency refers to the number of people that will be impacted. Because the resources are always limited, you will have to choose whether you prefer to have a higher reach or a higher frequency. The right balance is critical for your campaign. Keep in mind that a frequency of one, for the most part, will be a waste of resources. At the same time, reaching the same audience over and over may not give you the results that you are hoping to achieve because of saturation. Normally, theory talks about an average frequency of three to have some effect; of course, that number can vary a lot depending on the circumstances.

We can divide traditional advertising media into four main categories: TV, radio, Out-of-home advertising, and print media. In the next table, you will see some of the advantages and disadvantages of each of these.

Media	Advantage	Disadvantage
TV	High reach Cost per contact is low Have the capability to tell stories with images and sound	High total cost of the ad Competition for the customer attention is high Channel change or attention going to other media during ads Losing audience to streaming services, such as Netflix
Radio	High segmentation possible Most suited for local offers Mobile—listen anywhere Sound and music	Low attention level as most of the time people are doing something else at the same time National audiences can be difficult to reach
Out-of-Home	Very geo-segmented Low cost per impression High frequency Large visuals possible High creativity possible	The exposure time is very short, so the messages have to be brief
Print Media	Geographic selectivity High segmentations in magazines Can work for coupons or other sales promotions	Buying procedures can be a hassle Aging readership Little flexibility

Television

Probably the most well-known media is television, or TV. It has the advantage of being able to tell a story with images and audio, and at the same time, it can usually be found in the customer's home, in a living room, bedrooms, and/or kitchen. Not only that, but it is the traditional media with the highest reach. Because of this, it has a lower Cost-per-Contact (CPC) or contact per person.

Even with a low CPC, TV is still generally the most costly media. For example, 30 seconds of advertising during a Super Bowl costs a little over 5 million dollars. Because around 103 million people saw it in 2018, the CPC is about $20 USD; however, as a brand you still need to have the 5 million dollars to pay for the ad.

Another problem with TV is that so many commercials make it difficult for the consumer to remember and pay attention to yours. On top of that, changing channels during the commercial slot is extremely easy. Also, as we previously discussed, most of the time the customer will be watching something else in addition to the TV, so they will likely switch their attention more fully during advertising. In addition, traditional TV channels are losing audiences at a high rate to streaming services.

TV can use some of the interactions with digital as an opportunity for expansion; for example, a commercial aired on TV can then be promoted on YouTube or vice versa.

Measuring TV

The main method to measure TV advertising historically has been through ratings. Your favorite TV shows are often cancelled when they have low ratings.

A Super Bowl TV commercial costs around 5 million dollars; this is around $20 USD per contact.

The rating is the number of TVs on a specific television show divided by the numbers of TVs in the market. Nationally, this is typically determined by Nielsen with a People Meter and/or with a Set Meter. These are meters that are connected to a sample panel of TVs (Nielsen, 2019).

Local TV rating is measured using similar methods and is divided by Designated Market Area, or DMA. Not every DMA possesses People or Set Meters, so sometimes other techniques are used to determine who is watching what. A DMA is defined as a "geographic area where most of the population has the ability to receive the same media content" (Mediatracks, 2019).

The Top Five DMAs are (IDEM):

1. New York with 7,100,300 TV homes representing 6.441% of the US
2. Los Angeles with 5,276,600 TV homes representing 4.786% of the US
3. Chicago with 3,251,370 TV homes representing 2.949% of the US
4. Philadelphia with 2,816,850 TV homes representing 2.555% of the US
5. Dallas/Ft. Worth with 2,622,070 TV homes representing 2.378% of the US

A new element used to measure TV advertising is TV attribution. This is a method based on algorithms and machines learning to understand consumer behavior related to actions you might take regarding a product after watching a TV ad. Questions are raised like: Did the ad trigger searches for the productor visits to the Website? Did it trigger product orders? These can be answered with a TV attribution system. One of the many companies offering TV attribution is Google, within the Google Analytics services.

Suggested Video: Google Attribution 360: TV Attribution

Radio

Radio is a very mobile media. Even if you normally use Spotify or Apple Music or some other music streaming service, you may still hear radio from time to time. Most likely this is as a companion when you are driving or doing some other activity.

Radio has a good segmentation potential, as many radios are geared toward particular segments of music that are related to specific demographics and/or psychographics. Rock radio stations for example have a different target than

Radio usually has a low scope of attention, as the audience is often doing something else at the same time.

classical music radio stations. This is also true in terms of geo-segmentation, as most radio stations have a local audience.

It is, however, important to note that most of the time, the audience will be concentrating on a different task at the same time that the radio is on; this will limit the level of attention given to the radio.

Out-of-Home

As the name suggests, out-of-home (OOH) refers to advertising that reaches the audience when they are not at home. Some of the most used OOH resources are billboards, but the term also refers to advertising at bus stops, mobile billboards (on cars, or even bicycles), posters, brochure distribution, or even digital outdoor ads, such as on a kiosk, gas station screen, and many others.

OOH is a media that allows for high creativity. From the possibility to interact with consumers in digital OOH to the high formats of highway billboards, OOH advertising allows the marketer to be creative. Keep in mind though that most OOH ads have a limited time of exposure so the message has be very clear and short.

One of the most used OOH advertising resources is bus stops.

In general OOH advertising has proven to have a high frequency. Many people will pass by the same spot more than once a day, so there's a good audience; however, the reach is not as high as that in other media. In terms of segmentation, it does allow precise geographical segmentation but you will not be able to use many other segmenting variables.

Print Media

Magazines and newspaper are two of the most important forms of print media; both of them have similar characteristics but they are also different.

In term of segmentation, both of them allow high geographic segmentation. Magazines have the possibility of thematic or psychographic segmentation, as many magazines specialize in lifestyles, sports, or other categories.

As you may guess, newspapers readership is declining, and the loyal audience is aging. Many newspapers today are using digital platforms. The same is partially true for magazines, even though their audience decline is not as high as that for newspapers.

One important difference is the quality of the print. Often magazines will be full color and newspapers are not. This is something to consider when advertising.

Traditionally, newspaper have had the trust advantage; people used to believe that if something was in the newspaper, it was true. This is also something that has been decreasing with time.

Another important difference to mention between newspapers and magazines is the lifespan of the printed piece. Most of the time newspapers will last a day and then will be discarded; however, you can still read 5-year-old magazines in your dentist office.

Choosing an Advertising Agency

Before ending this chapter, we cannot forget to talk about advertising agencies, as most of the time they are the ones that will implement the advertising strategies. Some of the decisions that you will have to make before choosing an ad agency are discussed below:

- **In-House or external?** Not all companies use an external ad agency; some companies, such as Pepsi Co., use in-house agencies. In-house agencies have the advantage of working directly with the brand with faster input and feedback; however, they can lack the outsider perspective of external agencies.

- **Full-service or niche?** Do you want an ad agency that specializes in, for example, TV, digital or another media? Or do you want a full-service agency for all your IMC needs? The answer will depend on your particular needs and organizational structure.

- **What's the point?** What do you want from the ad agency? Need a branding strategy? Or to execute a perfect design? Do you want an agency that can help you get insight from the consumer or one that has the most creative talents? Depending on your needs, some agencies can be better suited than others.

- **Media capabilities:** Part of the previous point is how much media buying would you need? Do you need national or local media? Two elements of this are important: the media planning know–how and the media buying (negotiation) capabilities.

- **Small or large:** Bigger is not always better. A small client can have a hard time getting attention from a big agency. Consider the potential relationship with the account executive before deciding.

- **Experience:** Many companies look for agencies with experience in the industry. This could be a good idea but could also be limiting. An agency with experience outside the brand domain might be able to import better practices and ideas. Keep in mind also that ethically an ad agency should not work with two competitive companies at the same time.

- **Cost:** Don't just look at the direct cost, but also the overall price structure; determine if any agencies can help save you money in media buying, for example.

- **How many to invite to the party:** If you have studied all the other factors, you shouldn't come up with a very long list of initial agencies to talk to. Keep in mind that competing for your account has a cost—mostly in human resources hour but also maybe in productions and trips—for the agencies.

References

Allan, D. (2006). Effects of popular music in advertising on attention and memory. *Journal of Advertising Research, 46*(4), 434–444.

Chiang, K.-P., Chan, A., & Milan, R. (2018). Social marketing and advertising appeals: On perception and intention to purchase condoms among college students. *International Journal of Healthcare Management, 11*(2), 71–78. doi:10.1080/20479700.2016.1266149

Chung, H., & Zhao, X. (2003). Humour effect on memory and attitude: Moderating role of product involvement. *International Journal of Advertising, 22*(1), 117–144. doi:10.1080/02650487.2003.11072842

Clow, K., & Baack, D. (2018). *Integrated Advertising, Promotion, and Marketing Communications* (8 ed.).

Kellaris, J. J., & Cox, A. D. (1989). The effects of background music in advertising: A reassessment. *Journal of Consumer Research, 16*(1), 113–118.

Mediatracks (2019). Nielsen DMA Rankings 2019. Retrieved from https://mediatracks.com/resources/nielsen-dma-rankings-2019/

Nielsen. (2015). I second that emotion: The emotive power of music in advertising. Retrieved from https://www.nielsen.com/us/en/insights/news/2015/i-second-that-emotion-the-emotive-power-of-music-in-advertising.html

Nielsen. (2019). Nielse, ratings academy. Retrieved from http://ratingsacademy.nielsen.com/media-overview/panels

Reinartz, W., & Saffert, P. (2013). Creativity in advertising: When it works and when it doesn't. *Harvard Business Review, 91*(6), 106–112.

Taylor, C. (2019). Are Sexy Super Bowl Ads a Thing of the Past? Retrieved from https://www.forbes.com/sites/charlesrtaylor/2019/02/01/are-sexy-super-bowl-ads-a-thing-of-the-past/#5e3fe4723359

Weinberger, M. G., & Gulas, C. S. (1992). The impact of humor in advertising: A review. *Journal of Advertising, 21*(4), 35–59.

Wirtz, J. G., Sparks, J. V., & Zimbres, T. M. (2018). The effect of exposure to sexual appeals in advertisements on memory, attitude, and purchase intention: A meta-analytic review. *International Journal of Advertising, 37*(2), 168–198.

Yalch, R. F. (1991). Memory in a jingle jungle: Music as a mnemonic device in communicating advertising slogans. *Journal of Applied Psychology, 76*(2), 268.

Chapter 7
The Digital Brand

A connected world needs connected marketing.

© SFIO CRACHO/Shutterstock.com

The digital world today is mixed with the off-line world., Brands need to understand how to live in this new world. In this chapter, we analyze the relevance of the digital brand, then go further in discussing online advertising, in-bound and out-bound marketing, content marketing, and mobile marketing.

Learning Objectives for This Chapter:

- Discuss the importance of digital marketing.
- Recognize the different elements of online advertising.
- Distinguish between in-bound and out-bound marketing and when to use each of them.
- Distinguish the elements of a Search Engine Optimization (SEO) strategy.
- Be able to create a marketing content strategy.
- Differentiate the strategies in mobile marketing.

The Digital Revolution

Digital media, is defined by the marketing dictionary as follows:

"**Digital media** includes any **online or digital means of transmitting marketing** communications. Digital media currently includes—but is not limited to—websites, social networking environments, search engine ads, banner ads, email communications, streaming audio and video, online gaming, and mobile services" (marketing-dictionary.org).

As we have discussed in previous chapters, the eruption of digital media has changed the playing field of marketing in general and of marketing communication specifically.

Some of these changes that were already discussed in Chapters 1 and 2 are related to the consumer and the consumer journey. Other changes, however, are about brand interaction with the consumer, as well as brand management, planning, and measurement of success.

Digital media is everywhere at every moment! Think about the "relationship" that you have with your phone —the backbone of media in the digital field—you go to bed with it and it's probably the first thing that you look at in the morning. You have it with you all day long, and it is completely personalized to you. With it, you have your music, money, videos, games, and study material, all in your pocket.

Today, 98% of the adults in the US have access to the Internet (PewResearchCenter, 2018a), and 77% have some type of smartphone (PewResearchCenter, 2018b). While marketers used to say that TV was able to enter the bedroom of target families, digital and mobile advertising is able to enter the pocket. This not only means that we can target users everywhere, but also that, with the right tools, we can track user insights and behaviors.

This can also be translated to an exploding amount of data and insights, not only from mobile sources but also from social media, point of sales platforms, the Internet of Things, and more. The big challenge today with big data is how to process, read, and be able to manage all of these different sources of data.

The real-time effect is not just a data issue, it is also a planning and execution factor. While with traditional advertising you may have had months to prepare a message, today, with social media, marketers are interacting in real time with consumers. Not only that but often consumers are the ones creating content about the brand with brand reviews or Tweets about an interaction with a brand; these things lead to less control from a marketing perspective. Today, the goal is to think in terms of influence not message control.

The number of new digital platforms and the amount of messaging, brand related or not, makes cyberspace a very cluttered place, were only good and differentiated content will hold domain.

Online Advertising

Different methods can be used online for marketing purposes. Some of these methods are similar to what we normally do in traditional advertising but are adapted for online use. Some of these methods include:

- Display Advertising
- Native Ads and Sponsored Content
- E-mail Marketing
- Video Advertising
- Search Engine Marketing (SEM)

Other methods are more complex, and we will explain them later in this chapter. For now, let's take a look at the following online advertising tools.

Display Advertising

The most traditional and probably the first online advertising method is known as display advertising. Among this type of advertising we can find banners on Websites, pop-up advertising, and more.

Display ads can be contextually targeted depending on the Website where they will be displayed. Today's technology also allows us to *re-target* customers with display ads or even use behavioral targeting.

Display ads are considered *obstructionist* marketing. Keep in mind that some literature consider these types of ads to be annoying to customers, and even can be damaging for sales if not used correctly (Goldfarb & Tucker, 2011).

Display advertising is very common on Websites.

© Rawpixel.com/Shutterstock.com

Native Ads and Sponsored Content

Another type of online advertising is native ads. This is advertising that is set up with the same look as the native content on a site, so it doesn't look like an ad. One particular type of native ad is called **sponsored content**; this is content on a site that is paid for by a brand. For example, a credit card company might have a paid article on a news-based Website about "How to save money at Christmas."

Both native ads and sponsored content have to clearly disclose the fact that they are paid for by the brand. This, of course, can discourage users; however, a well thought-out native ad and specific and relevant sponsored content can be effective tools in your IMC mix.

In a Web portal, native ads will look exactly like the native content of the site; however, they have to clearly state that they are paid advertising.

© Kaspars Grinvalds/Shutterstock.com

E-mail Marketing

E-Mail marketing is an important part of marketing in most of today's modern campaigns. Used correctly and with the correct technological support, e-mail marketing allows brands to target very specifically to the customer, considering variables, such as:

- Online behavior of the user; for example, prospects that have looked at a particular type of products or services, such as families shopping for vacations rentals.
- Demographics of the customer
- Re-targeting customers that have previously shopped a site; for example, in cases of abandoned shopping carts
- Targeting users that could be interested in a specific event

- Targeting users in specific weather situations
- Geo-targeting customers in micro-target locations

Platforms, such as Hubspot, can help you mass personalize e-mails, as well as run some A/B testing. The use of marketing automation can also be a good mix with e-mail campaigns.

Analytics and metrics are an important part of e-mail marketing, as they can help you understand the effectiveness of your campaign and where and how you are attracting sales or marketing leads to your pipeline. One important thing to consider when designing an e-mail campaign is to include a call-for-action, such as a discount that leads to a landing page or free content. This will give your campaign the ability to track results. Some of the metrics that stand out when measuring the success of e-mail campaigns are e-mail open rates and clickthrough rates. Marketers should also consider having some type of conversion rates in the pipeline.

Another recommendation for e-mail campaigns is A/B testing; this is when you test two variations of an e-mail sent to similar targets to see which is the most effective strategy. A/B testing is very useful in e-mail marketing as well as in many other types of digital marketing.

A final issue to consider, in e-mail marketing, is **permission marketing.**

Permission marketing focuses on getting authorization from the client to communicate with them. It has been proven that the customer is much more willing to open e-mails that come from services that he or she has subscribed to over e-mails that are sent without our permission(Chang, Rizal & Amin, 2013).

This is a strategic and effective element, not necessarily a legal issue. Although in many countries brands do need to have an opt-in from the consumer to initiate contact, in the US brands just need to supply an opt-out alternative in the message for e-mail campaigns.

Permission marketing should create attractive alternatives for the customer to be interested in engaging in and receiving brand communications.

Video Advertising

With so many streaming services and social media platforms providing some type of video access, it is no surprise that video content is an important tool for IMC. YouTube, Facebook, Twitter, Instagram, LinkedIn, Snapchat—all of these offer some type of video advertising alternative. There's also the possibility of advertising on Hulu, HBO Go, or other streaming channels. In addition, other potential places for online videos include blogs and various Websites.

There are many categories of video ads online; three of the most common ones are discussed below (Jabbari, 2017):

- **In-stream ads:** These are videos that play within another video. Three subcategories of in-stream ads exist: (a) pre-roll, the ad is played at the beginning of the video; (b) mid-roll, the ad is played at the middle of the video; and (c) post-roll, the ad is played after the video content. It is important to note that the effectiveness of post-roll ads is low, as the audience has no motivation to continue viewing. Mid-roll ads usually have greater engagement; however, some controversy exists because of the interruptive element.
- **In-read ads:** These videos appear when you are scrolling a Website. A video will appear within the text, and the content will begin playing without sound. These types of videos also are considered interruptive; however, the audience has the control to continue playing the video or stop it.
- **In-banner video ads:** These are videos that are embedded in a Website banner; they are the least effectives type of videos.

These are just three of the different types of current video ads; every day they evolve with the technology. Something to consider when designing a video ad is that normally you will have to engage the user fast. In in-stream ads, for example, the user may have the chance to skip the video after a few seconds; in in-read ads, the consumer can decide to stop watching the ad just after a few frames.

It is important to mention that online video marketing is bigger than just video ads.

Search Engine Marketing

The concept of Search Engine Marketing (SEM) is very close to the concept of Search Engine Optimization (SEO). As you can guess, both are related to search engines, or specifically how the customer can find your service easily when using a search engine and looking for a word that is related to your offering. In this way SEO will deal with the organic (non-paid) appearance in search engines and SEM will deal with the paid advertising in search engines. In this part of the book, we will discuss SEM; later in this chapter, we will discuss SEO.

To discuss SEM, we will focus on Google Advertising services (https://ads.google.com), as it is the most used search engine in the world. How-

Millions of people rely on Google for searches each day. Marketers can advertise offerings to appear with specific words searched.

ever, many of the other search engines use similar methods. To effectively advertise on Google, the marketer must at least follow the steps listed below:

1. Create keywords: You can use the keyword planner or other tools, such as Google Trends, to decide what words will make the most sense to use in your advertising. To choose the words, think as a customer might: ask yourself what words might someone with a need or want matching your offering search for. Someone with a cold, for example, might look for "tips to fight a cold" instead of using the word "medicine."

2. Decide how much to bid on keywords and your campaign budget: Keep in mind that every time someone looks for a concept, Google decides what advertisers to show based on two specific factors: (1) an auction where the advertiser that bid a higher price on a word is ranked higher, and (2) a quality score that is calculated according to how relevant your ad and Webpage are to the consumer that is searching. When deciding on your budget, you need to determine how much to bid on a word(hopefully slightly higher than your competition) and how much to allocate for the full campaign.

3. Design the ad and landing page: As mentioned above, the quality score of your ad and your Webpage is important. The design of the ad is also critical for the consumer to decide to actually click through it; so, you want to choose the right text, image, and colors. Another important element to design is the landing page. This is the page that the ad leads to; you don't want the ad to lead to your homepage for many reasons. You want a landing page that has a specific objective in mind, is related to your ad, and limits extra navigation. This page should contain a call to action (CAT); this will make it easier to measure conversion rates and the effectives of the ad (Meher, 2017). You can test your ad and/or your landing pages with A/B testing.

4. Launching campaign and measuring results. Don't forget to track your ad; from reach to conversion rates and specific target effectiveness, in Google you can follow all of these things using Google Analytics.

In-Bound and Out-Bound Marketing

With the exception of SEM, all of the efforts in advertising online are examples of what we call **out-bound marketing**. This is basically a method of going out and hunting for clients, sometimes even interrupting them. A different approach, made possible with new technology is **in-bound marketing**, which is based on making it easier for the customer to find us when they need us. There are two well-known and effective types of in-bound marketing. One of these is **Search Engine Optimization**, which focuses on making it easier for consumers to find your Website when they are using a search engine.

The second one is **content marketing**. Content marketing focuses on creating brand content, managing that content, and encouraging users to develop and share additional content related to the brand. The creation of brand content can attract users to the brand site because of the content instead of just the offering.

Google Analytics can track not only the performance of your Google ads but also the performance of your Webpage.

© WDnet Creation/Shutterstock.com

Search Engine Optimization (SEO)

When a consumer looks for something related to your offering, you want to appear among the first results, or at least on the first page of results. But how do you step up in the search engine rating? One way to appear first was already discussed and that is paying for it; however, another way is to appear organically; this is called SEO.

Search Engines, such as Google, look for three elements to rank a Webpage: trust, authority, and relevance (Clarke, 2018). **Trust** is about the quality of the content on the Website; **authority** indicates how well the Website is positioned in relationship to other Websites and social media; and **relevance** matches how relevant the content of the Website is to

People typically concentrate their attention on the first page of results in Google; this is why SEO is so important.

© Africa Studio/Shutterstock.com

the search initiated by the user. But how can you increase the trust, authority, and **relevance** of your Website? Different methods are appropriate for this; here are some examples:

Are you in Google? The first step is maybe the most obvious. You need to determine if your Website appears in Google at all. To know this you have to google "site:yourdomain" and see if every page that you want to appear in your domain is there.

Keyword research: As with SEM, an important step in SEO is to research the potential keywords that you want your site to appear on. Type in each keyword and note how or whether your page appears. This is going to be important for the next step.

In-page SEO: In SEO not all the factors are internal or in-page factors; however, a series of modifications to your own Webpage will help optimize your SEO. The first important issue to consider is that the words you use are imperative for the relevance factor. So, whatever content you create, the words in use have to be strategically placed to help *googlebots* find your page when someone is looking for that type of content. However, it is not just the words that you use that is relevant but also the creation of **quality content.**

Another important aspect to consider is your use of **meta tags**. These are words embedded in your page HTML code. not necessarily visible to the human eye. There are varying viewpoints on how important meta tags are for today's SEO. It's possible that, they are not extremely relevant; however, meta tag words are not difficult to set up so should be a part of your SEO strategy.

Other in-page modifications are a little more technical. For example, you should avoid pages with **duplicate content** (two pages under the same domain with the same or very similar content) because this will negatively impact your SEO. Duplicate content can sometimes be an issue on platforms like Wordpress. Another technical element to consider is the creation of a **sitemap**; this is a XML file that will inform *googlebots* where to look and how to rank certain pages in relation with the other pages in your domain. Both of these elements, sitemaps and avoiding duplicate content, as well as most of the other in-page factors can be worked on with an SEO Optimizer.

Mobile optimization: One of the newest important factors in SEO is mobile optimization; this ensures that a Website will be well adapted to a mobile screen. Nowadays, Google has a policy called "Mobile First" that gives the highest ranking to Websites that are optimized for mobile use. You can test the optimization of a Website for mobile use in https://search.google.com/test/mobile-friendly or other similar systems.

Strategic link building: Another element that most search engines take into consideration is the network of links pointing to your site. In other words, it is not only important how many external links (links that are not in your domain) link back to your Website but also the quality of those domains. Google uses a rating known as PageRank to calculate the number/quality of back links pointing to a site. In th Google Analytics you can track the sites that link to your page.

Once you know what pages link to your page, you need to start building a better base of links. Good quality content is crucial, as well as working actively to promote that content. An alternative to promoting content and get-

Most searches these days are done on a smartphone, so Google now has a Mobile First policy for SEO.

© Denys Prykhodov/Shutterstock.com

ting backlinks is a tool called HARO (Help a Reporter Out), where bloggers and journalists ask for quotes or interviews about different subjects. Often, if your content is selected, they will add a link on their Website back to yours, recognizing the source. We will explore more about HARO in Chapter 9 in the PR section.

A word of caution: in the market of backlink building for SEOs, there are many companies that offer services to get more links. While some of these companies are legitimate and will do an organic work, promoting the Website and its content, others sell bad quality links, spamming the comment section of thousands of blogs. Not only does this tactic not work today, but even worse, Google and other search engines have the technology to detect these cases and can punish or block the Websites involved. These types of practices violate search engines terms of services, and are known as Black Hat SEOs.

Application Exercise:

Choose any Website and then go to Google and look for a free SEO audit. Run the audit for your chosen Website and add your findings below:

Website:
Five most important conclusions from the report:

Content Marketing

At the heart of any digital marketing or social media campaign is content marketing, Bill Gates wrote an article in 1996 making a bold prediction (Bailey, 2010): Content will be king . Think about one of the largest corporations of today, for example, Disney World. What do most of the strategic business units of Disney have in common? Well, they either sell content or experience or both. And the content—movies, for example —inspires the experiences, such as in the parks or with related toys.

In marketing Phillip Kother said that "Content is the new ad and #hashtag is the new tagline" (Kotler, Kartajaya & Setiawan, 2016). This is the same Kotler who gave us the following definition of Content Marketing:

Disney Plus will serve as a distribution system for the giant content creation model of the different business units in Walt Disney Corp.

© Ivan Marc/Shutterstock.com

"Content marketing is a marketing approach that involves creating, curating, distributing, and amplifying content that is interesting, relevant, and useful to a clearly defined audience group in order to create conversations about the content." (Kotler et al., 2016, p. 121)

As you can see in this definition, content marketing is interested in the conversations around the content. Another important part of this definition is that content has to be interesting, relevant, and useful for a specific audience. Advertising is usually a direct call to buy the brand or at least feel something for the brand. Content marketing, however, is more about the consumer's interests, fears, and wants, giving the consumer content that is related to the brand but not necessarily about the brand.

While advertising tries to create a position in the mind of the prospect saying something about the brand, content marketing tries to do the same by telling them something of interest that creates a positive feeling about the brand. For example, a hospital can use advertising to promote the speed or high quality of the services that they provide; on the other hand, the same hospital will use content marketing to create articles to educate users on how to react in an emergency or how to detect the symptoms of a specific health issue. These articles will generate the idea that the hospital is an "expert" on those matters and may generate a feeling of good will regarding the hospital. Content marketing and advertising are valuable tools for IMC, and both can be used depending on the campaign objective.

Marketing content can be used to educate, inform, or entertain and can take the form of written articles, Tweets, videos, memes, pictures, or any other format. In marketing, content can be divided into two types: **brand generated content** and **user generated content**. In this chapter, we will focus on the steps for generating the first type; in the next chapter, we will focus more on the second type of content.

Kotler (2016) specified eight steps to create a good quality content strategy:

1. **Goal setting:** What is the goal of the campaign and how and what type of content can be useful to achieve it?

2. **Map the audience:** What is your target? What are their needs and wants, their interests, their fears? What do they talk about on social media?

3. **Content ideation and planning**: What themes are going to dominate your content? What is your brand voice and style? Wwhat will be the storyline or storylines?
4. **Content creation**: Who is going to create the content and how? Will it be done by a communications manager in house? An external agency? A mix?
5. **Content distribution**: How will we distribute the content? Through own digital media, paid or earn? Or in some type of mix as with an influencer strategy?
6. **Content amplification**: How do we make the content go viral? We will discuss this further in the next chapter.
7. **Content evaluation**: What are our metrics? How and when are we going to measure them?
8. **Content improvement**: After evaluation, what types of changes do we need to make to the planning?

You can use this list as a general guide, but each campaign will have its own requirements; also in addition, each form of digital media you use will generate more specific elements to consider. In the next chapter, we will examine some of these elements for the most relevant social media today.

Application Exercise:

Think about your favorite brand:

What type of content would you create for this brand?

Mobile Marketing

Before we conclude the chapter on digital marketing and before we move on to social media, we need to discuss a specific area of digital marketing that is very relevant today. This is mobile marketing.

As we stated earlier, mobile optimization is crucial today. The number of searches done through mobile devices has grown exponentially; the smartphone is with you everywhere and for everything. Mobile devices today:

- Have your music, movies, books, social media, and all your interests
- Can geo-track you, know where you are, or even predict where you are going to go according to your routing
- Can track your health, especially in combination with a smart watch
- Are devices for video, photo, and live streaming, where you can create content and share it with the world
- Have smart assistants and can recognize your voice; this technology is advancing at a high rate.
- Have sensors to understand altitude and positions of the phone
- Can be used as a wallet to pay for things and store documents and records
- Are game devices, planners, or any other tool that you may require according to the apps that you have downloaded
- Are a door of communication between the real world and the virtual world; for example, with QR codes, you can scan something and go to a Webpage, and with augmented reality you can add things that are not there to a reality.

Because of all of the above, other than the relevance of *Mobile First* for SEO, mobile as a marketing medium has many alternatives. Four of the most relevant or promising today are:

Mobile phones are with us at every moment.

SMS or MMS messaging: These types of messages have a better response in general than e-mails as they feel more personal. Also, because permission marketing is crucial, research has found that consumers respond better to SMS not only when they receive relevant information but also when they are familiar with the brand (Bakr, Tolba,& Meshreki, 2019). It is also important to note that, unlike e-mail campaigns, because the contact is through a phone, brands have to comply with the "Telephone Consumer Protection Act," and users have to opt-in before receiving these types of messages.

Apps marketing: Another potential use of mobile marketing is the creation of mobile apps for brands. Companies like L'Oreal, BMW, Nike, Corona, WalMart, Dominos, Verizon, and many others use app marketing as a communication channel. Of course, to that list, you can add many other brands that are in the app business, for example, Uber or AirBnB.

Even though we recognize the importance of mobile apps, 80% of all app users "churn" within three months (Vieira, 2017). This means that they will delete the app or unsubscribe to the service before three month of use. Not only to avoid being a part of this statistic, an ideal marketing app will create a link between the user and the brand. To do this, it is important that the app have some stimulus to engage the user in a constant use of the app. To achieve this, there four major areas that the brand should consider when designing an app (Eyal, 2014):

1. **Triggers:** What are the internal (motivations, need, and wants) and external (what gets the user's attention) triggers that will get the user to download the app?

2. **Actions:** The app has to present a faster or shorter way to get to a potential reward.

3. **Reward:** What is the reward for using the app? It needs to be fulfilling but also invite the user to want more of it.

4. **Investment:** What type of investment will the user have to put in to continue on the system? Buy something? Use the app more frequently? Recommend the app? As you can see, the question of investment is at the last stage. Think for a moment of the most popular mobile games; most of them are free to play; however, often they will encourage the user to buy extra material on-game after the player is engaged with the game.

Mobile geo-targeting systems: Another important element of mobile marketing is the ability to geo target the consumer, using the localization systems on the phone. In this way, today, for example, we can create a **geo-fence** using a phone's GPS. This is a virtual fence around the user that is used to identify when he or she is near a brand location so that the brand can send relevant messages and advertising. Another popular mechanism is the use of beacons; this is Bluetooth technology that will connect to phones when they are in close proximity. They are used today to send promotional messages to people that are in-store or very close to a store.

Mobile technology allows brands to communicate with the consumers when they are in close proximity to a store or in a specific geo-location.

Augmented Reality: Maybe one of the newest technologies that is starting to revolutionize current mobile marketing is Augmented Reality (AR). Smartphones now can be a tool for interaction between a virtual world and the real word, seeing what is not there. Brands like Ikea, Home Depot, and Sephora are using AR successfully.

Augmented reality has been used mostly for games, such as Pokémon Go, however, the technology has great potential for marketing.

References

Bailey, C. (2010). Content is king by Bill Gates. Retrieved from https://www.craigbailey.net/content-is-king-by-bill-gates/

Bakr, Y., Tolba, A., & Meshreki, H. (2019). Drivers of SMS advertising acceptance: A mixed-methods approach. *Journal of Research in Interactive Marketing, 13*(1), 96–118.

Chang, H., Rizal, H., & Amin, H. (2013). The determinants of consumer behavior towards email advertisement. *Internet Research, 23*(3), 316–337.

Clarke, A. (2018). *SEO 2018*.

Eyal, N. (2014). *Hooked: How to build habit-forming products:* Penguin UK.

Goldfarb, A., & Tucker, C. (2011). Online display advertising: Targeting and obtrusiveness. *Marketing Science, 30*(3), 389–404.

Jabbari, S. (2017). What are the Different Video Ad Formats Available? Retrieved from https://www.pulpix.com/insights/blog/what-are-different-video-ad-formats/

Kotler, P., Kartajaya, H., & Setiawan, I. (2016). *Marketing 4.0: Moving from traditional to digital:* John Wiley & Sons.

marketing-dictionary.org. (Ed.).

Meher, J. (2017). 9 Must-Haves for the Perfect Landing Page. Retrieved from https://blog.hubspot.com/blog/tabid/6307/bid/26866/9-must-haves-for-the-perfect-landing-page.aspx

PewResearchCenter. (2018a). Internet/Broadband Fact Sheet. Retrieved from https://www.pewinternet.org/fact-sheet/internet-broadband/

PewResearchCenter. (2018b). Mobile Fact Sheet. Retrieved from https://www.pewinternet.org/fact-sheet/mobile/

Vieira, A. (2017). Most app users churn within 3 months—Here's how to avoid becoming a statistic. Retrieved from https://www.thinkwithgoogle.com/marketing-resources/customer-lifetime-value-marketing-apps/

Chapter 8
The Social Brand

Social media dominates our social life today, but how to use it for marketing is a key question that this chapter will discuss.

© Twin Design/Shutterstock.com

Social media has revolutionized how brands communicate with customers and how customers communicate with them. This chapter analyzes the most used social media platforms and gives some ideas in terms of strategies to use in this important marketing vehicle.

Learning Objectives for This Chapter:

- Discuss the relevance of social media in the IMC mix.
- Identify the elements of the major social media platforms.
- Be able to build and design a social media presence for a brand.
- Differentiate social media strategies and how to use them.

Social Media Marketing

If the Internet changed things for consumers and marketers, the so-called Web 2.0 makes the changes even deeper. Social media allows the consumer to interact with brands on a daily basis and allows brands to interact with consumers in real time. People are now media in the form of social influencers, and their complaints can become viral, destroying a brand's reputation with a click of a button.

The reasons for using social media by a brand can be multiple. It is important to be clear on the objectives before embracing a social media strategy. Some of the possible reasons for using social media are to:

- Reach a new audience
- Complement the frequency of other media in the same target
- Interact with consumers and engage them with the brand
- Improve SEO and generate traffic to a Website
- Gather customer intelligence and customer insights
- Create a fan base or a community of consumers
- Generate sales and marketing leads
- Improve sales
- Improve brand equity

Many other reasons are possible, but these are the most common ones.

Social Media Today

Today we have many possibilities for social media channels. Each has specific purposes and objectives. Among the most popular social media outlets for marketers are Facebook, YouTube, Twitter, Instagram, Linked-In, and Snapchat. We will talk about all of these in this chapter.

Keep in mind that the list above is limited and marketers have many more possibilities available. Also, new social media sites are being introduced every day. Some of the other effective social media sites that can be used for marketing include **Pinterest,** more popular with women (Smith & Anderson, 2018) and very useful for clothing brands and other industries; **Reddit,** a great alternative for online communities and fan conversations; and **Taringa,** a very popular site in Latin America.

Other types of social platforms are messaging apps, such as WhatsApp, Skype, LINE, or Facebook Messaging. Marketing through messaging apps is still in development; however, marketers can use these for group messaging or direct communication with customers. Also, the use of AI messaging bots is becoming more popular every day for custumer services.

Facebook

With 1.56 billion daily active users on average for March 2019 (Facebook, 2019), Facebook is one of the largest social media sites, and it has had huge implications in the way many companies now approach marketing (Ramsaran-Fowdar, 2013).

One thing to consider with Facebook is that even though it is still the biggest and most used social media site, Gen Z and Millennials are more comfortable using other platforms, such as Instagram or Snapchat.

For marketers Facebook can be used in many ways; some of the most popular are Facebook pages, groups, events, and Facebook ads.

Facebook is the largest social media site.

© Denys Prykhodov/Shutterstock.com

Facebook pages may be the most used feature for marketers. These are free pages where brands can interact with users. Facebook pages can be used in many ways by brands: as a brand community, an information page, a customer service platform, and more.

In Facebook pages, brands can **post** text, videos, and images as well as create events and other activities on their pages. For a consumer to **receive a brand post**, the consumer has to follow or like the page or receive a link to it by a Facebook friend that has liked or shared the post. This type of reach is known as organic reach and it is free. However, the organic reach of Facebook pages has been declining recently because of changes in the algorithm that Facebook uses to decide what to show and what not to show to users. This, of course, has forced some companies to "boost" the post—a form of paid advertising that shows the post to more people.

Nevertheless, marketers shouldn't discard organic reach and, if important to the strategy, should attempt to create quality post content that can grow organically. Even if the decision is made to pay to boost a post, good quality content that is aligned to the strategy will perform better than bad quality content.

Some of the factors that can create better engagement in Facebook posts are listed below (Malhotra, Malhotra & See, 2013):

1. Use photos.
2. Be topical (use events, holidays, or other topics to engage the user).
3. Promote the brand and its products.
4. Share validation.
5. Educate the fans.
6. Humanize the brand; appeal to emotions.
7. Use of humor when appropriate.
8. Don't be afraid to ask to be liked or shared.

Facebook is a platform that is very data rich. When using Facebook pages, brands can track the performance of a post by simply checking Facebook Insights were page views, post reach, page likes, video view statistics, and other metrics are available. Also, the marketer can gain access to more detailed facts by downloading the data file in Insights—available separately for posts and pages—to review information, such as reach, views, likes, reaction type, un-follows, users ,and many other metrics.

As we discussed previously, reaching users organically is one path on Facebook. However, another option is paying for it; marketers can pay on Facebook to boost a particular post or event. This is the simple and less customizable paid option. Another

Page and post data can be accessed in Facebook Insights.

© PixieMe/Shutterstock.com

more complex option is **Facebook ads.** With ads, brands can choose where their ad will appear—in a mobile feed, for example, or on a desktop. They can also choose whether it will just be on Facebook or also on Instagram.

Facebook ads also gives the brand the opportunity to choose the objective of the campaign. In this way, they can optimize the performance. Maybe the biggest advantage of Facebook ads, however, is the capability to micro-segment its audience, for example, by location, age, gender, language, or other more specific demographics, interests, or behaviors. Also, the audience can be more customizable, including factors like:

- **Website traffic:** Target people that visit your Website and/or that took specific actions on the Website, such as leaving products in the cart (re-targeting)
- **App activity:** Target people using your app or who have done specific actions inside of the app.
- **Off-line activity and database:** Uploading specific databases inside Facebook
- **Others:** Tracking Instagram, video, or Facebook behaviors per the user

Finally, customizable audiences can also be determined with a tool called *Lookalike*. This allow brands to create audiences similar to the current followers of the brand's Facebook page.

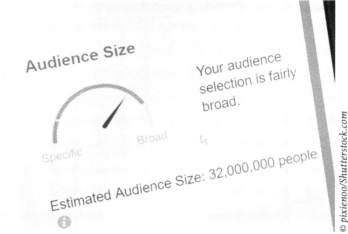

When using Facebook ads, the audience is customizable; you don't want to be too broad, but you still need to target a relatively important size of an audience.

YouTube

Another one of the biggest social media sites is YouTube; 73% of US adults say that they use YouTube (Smith & Anderson, 2018). Just like Facebook, YouTube can be used in many ways for brands. Some of these include having its own YouTube channel; partnering with others, including influencers (which we will talk about further in this chapter); or using paid advertising.

When creating content for YouTube, the brand has to take into consideration the many ways that users use YouTube; these include:

- **Self-learning:** These videos show how to fix something in the house or car or how to use various software.
- **Know about a product before buying:** Consumer reviews or unboxing of products are very popular.
- **Entertainment:** Don't forget that YouTube is an entertainment platform. Funny and entertaining videos can cause a great viral effect.

YouTube has become in a great place for self-learning; this represents a great marketing opportunity.

In terms of paid possibilities, according to YouTube, five types of advertising are possible in the platform:

- **Skippable in-stream ads:** Video ads that play before, during, or after another video. The video can usually be skipped after 5 seconds. Brands pay only for the videos that users interact with or if they watch the entire video (or at least 30 seconds if video is longer than that).
- **Non-skippable in-stream ads:** Video ads that play before, during, or after another video. These videos cannot be skipped and normally last 15 seconds.
- **Bumper ads:** Short video ads that play before, during, or after another video. These videos cannot be skipped, but they are only 6 seconds or shorter.

- **Video discovery ads:** YouTube video that will appear in YouTube searches, alongside related videos or in the YouTube mobile homepage. The user will have to click to see the videos.
- **Outstream ads:** This type of ad is hosted by YouTube but will not appear on YouTube. It appears on partner sites. These video ads are shown on mobile devices (tablets and smartphones) and begin playing with the sound off when the user is scrolling through videos.

As with Facebook, YouTube has great metrics. Some of them are:

- Impressions: Every time the ad is shown
- Unique reach: Number of people who saw the ad
- View rate: Rate of people who watched the video vs. the number of times it was shown
- Watch time: Total amount of time the video was watched
- Engagement: Interaction of users with the video
- Video viewership: Percentage of the video viewed by the consumer

Twitter

Even tough Twitter may not be as big as Facebook or YouTube, its public character acts as a resonance chamber. Many of the tweets from famous people, politicians, or companies appear later on in the news or generate some type of buzz effect. Of course, this buzz can be either negative or positive. That's why brands need to be sure to be using Twitter in the right way and that they understand its importance and place in the IMC mix.

Just like the previous social media outlets we have discussed so far, Twitter can be used organically by posting tweets and interacting with other users. It also offers paid advertising or a promotional mode that will promote the tweets on an account.

Celebrities, business people, politicians, and brands use Twitter to communicate directly with an audience.

Some recommendations when posting Twitter for marketing campaigns come from an official Twitter blog (Alton, 2017):

- Create mini-campaigns from long-form content; this could be, for example, pieces of a book, a movie, or other content.
- Use Twitter polls and ask questions to interact with users.
- Go cross-channel by mining your other content; Twitter can be a good resonance chamber for material posted in YouTube, Facebook, Instagram, or blogs.
- Include images and visual elements in your tweets.
- Develop a themed content series, where you can include stories of customers, facts about the product or industry, or introduce employees, leaders, or others.
- Use #hashtags for tracking and to stimulate the conversation.

As we mentioned above, the use of hashtags should be an integral part of a Twitter campaign. This is not just the use of brand-created hashtags but also the incorporation of trending topics. Jumping to a trending topic hashtag however, has to done carefully and with a clear understanding of the conversation. One story that exemplifies the risk of this involves the pizza brand DiGiorno. They jumped into the hashtag #whyistayed, Tweeting "cause you had Pizza." The problem? The conversation was about domestic violence; women were telling their stories with the mentioned hashtag. DiGiorno not only had to erase the tweet, explaining that they weren't aware of the tone of the conversation, but they also had to use a great amount of time apologizing for the tweet.

Some of the metrics available in Twitter are: impressions, profile visits, engagement and engagement rates, audience demographics, lifestyle, and behavior.

Instagram

Owned by Facebook Inc., Instagram has become one of the most popular sites for young people (Smith & Anderson, 2018). Due to its highly visual content, it serves as a good place for many brands. One of the most used strategies on Instagram is the use of influencers. We will discuss this further in this chapter. Here brands can create their own accounts and post their own content as well as pay for advertising. **Paid advertising** on Instagram is managed from the Facebook ads page and works in a similar way.

As a highly graphic site, Instagram is perfect for brands that want to connect to their customers visually.

As we mentioned before, Instagram is very visual, so the brand content must be esthetic. Just as with Facebook, interacting with users through contests and questions works very well on Instagram.

To use Instagram Insights, brands have to have a business account; data on Instagram is grouped in three distinct sets of metrics:

- Activity: People that interact and discover the account
- Content: Data about the performance of posts, stories, and paid ads
- Audience: Followers and audience data

LinkedIn

LinkedIn is mostly popular among college graduates and high-income households (Smith & Anderson, 2018). Use of this platform by brands and companies is usually done by human resources for recruitment purpose. However, its professional outlook offers some strong possibilities for marketing, especially, but not only, in B2B marketing. In this context, LinkedIn is probably one of the most useful sites for **sales lead generation**.

LinkedIn also has paid ads and post-boosting options. Some of the paid options include native ads, sponsored InMail, text ads, and more. The performance metrics on this platform are related to conversions and audience analytics.

Snapchat

The new kid on the block, Snapchat, has a strong growth with young adults (Smith & Anderson, 2018). Criticized for its constant changes that make the marketer learning process somehow more difficult, Snapchat's esthetics and story-telling model has influenced changes in other players in social media, such as Facebook and Instagram.

A big innovation in Snapchat is the native use of augmented reality; this is something that businesses can use when creating content. In terms of paid advertising, Snapchat offers many possibilities; some of them include story ads, six-second commercials, and AR lenses and filters that users can interact with.

Building a Social Media Presence

Just as with any other media, using social media should be a well-planned, well-crafted, and carefully executed activity, where every decisions made is in response to the overall IMC strategy. Many companies assume that a social media strategy consists of just setting up a Twitter or Facebook account and hoping for the best. Of course, that is not the professional way to do it.

Marketers planning to work with social media should at least determine these things:

1. **Objectives:** What objectives are set that involve the use of social media? Do you want more reach? More engagement? Frequency of the message? To create fans? And how do those objectives relate to the biggest IMC objectives?

2. **Brand personality:** We discussed brand personality and brand voice in previous chapters. These definitions are crucial for social media. How will the brand behave? How will it interact with consumers? Will it be funny or serious?

3. **Social media mix:** What forms of social media will the brand use? There's no need to use all of them, just the ones that the brand can be active in and that are in line with the objectives and brand persona. However, a brand may want to create a profile and reserve the brand name in all the major SM sites to prevent an incorrect use of the brand. Once set up, the brand does not have to actively use them all.

4. **Content and SM strategy:** It's important to determine how the content will be created and what social media strategies the brand will be using. We will discuss some of these later in the chapter.

5. **Metrics and feedback:** How are we going to measure social media results and what might we learn in each step?

Strategies for Social Media

Using social media is not just about choosing the right place. Different strategies can be implemented across various platforms. Some of them have been discussed already when explaining each of the major platforms, such as, for example, paid advertising in social media. Other options can be used across platforms; some of the most used today are:

- Content management and user-generated content
- Online brand communities
- Influencer marketing
- Viral marketing
- Growth hacking/marketing

We will examine these strategies in the next part of this chapter.

Content Management and User-Generated Content

As we mentioned in Chapter 7, content marketing is crucial, not only for social media, but also for all types of digital marketing. Two elements of content marketing are especially relevant when talking about social media. We haven't gone into details on these yet; however, these include how to make the brand content go viral and how to manage and promote positive user-generated content (U-GC).

Creating **viral marketing** content is one of the most ambitious tasks that a marketer can embrace. High creativity, strategic thinking, and consumer insights are needed. Also, sometimes just a little bit of luck is necessary. A successful viral campaign can gain thousands or millions in the way of free reach. But what are some of the elements that make content go viral? Professor Jonah Berger, after much research on messages that have gone viral, came up with a series of elements that are key to making content viral. He called it the STEPPS process (Berger, 2016):

- **Social currency.** We share things that make us look good. People, for example, might recommend an elegant restaurant just to show that they belong in it, not necessarily because they loved the food.
- **Triggers.** Some context can help trigger other ideas. For example, Mars bar sales spiked in 1997 when NASA's Pathfinder mission explored the red planet. The song "Friday" by Rebecca Black usually has its playing peaks on Fridays.
- **Emotion.** People share what is important to them; high arousal leads to high sharing.
- **Public.** People tend to follow others; this is why if a restaurant is full of people, others will follow. This also explains why survey promotion is so important in political marketing.
- **Practical.** As humans we like to give advice. If something is practical and we believe it can help others, we may be tempted to share.
- **Stories.** As we discussed before, stories always triumph over facts. People listen to and share stories over facts.

Rebecca Black's song, "Friday," wasn't particularly good quality music; however, it was a hit on YouTube, when? Every Friday.

Suggested Video: Contagious! Why things catch on.

Apart from creating viral content, social media can be used to promote and stimulate user-generated content (U-GC); this is any type of content created by the consumer, ranging from consumer reviews, to YouTube videos using a product, to Twitter posts complaining about a service, to a picture of a plate of food from a restaurant posted on Instagram.

Even though U-GC will be created with or without brand participation, the brand should attempt to positively influence the content. Some of the tactics that can be used are listed below:

- **Create and promote a contest:** For example, some brands hold Instagram contests for the best picture of the product or something similar.
- **Ask for feedback:** Don't be afraid to ask the consumer for feedback or to participate in an online conversation. Many companies invite the consumer to review their products or services online.
- **Share U-GC:** If people tend to post images or content that is positive and associated with your brand, share it. Other people will follow.
- **Interact and answer:** Social M=media is set up for interaction. If people interact with a brand and the brand doesn't respond, most people will simply stop interacting with the brand.
- **Crowdsourcing:** Many platforms of crowdsourcing are now available; this is a way of asking the consumer to solve a problem for you. New innovations or even suggestions on how to promote a product are possible responses.
- **Follow and Listen:** Don't forget to listen to what people are saying and respond to that feedback in your strategy.

Online Brand Community

Brands, such as Harley-Davidson, Jeep, and Porsche have had brand communities many years before the online world was a thing. It is, however, this new virtual scenario and especially social media sites like Facebook that have influenced the emergence of Online Brand Communities (OBC) for other brands. These OBCs can emerge in different ways. For example, some are created by fans, such as the many fan pages for Marvel Avengers or pages for products, such as the Porsche Macan Owners Club (PMOC). Also, brand communities can be created by the brand itself, such as the Red Bull Facebook page. Some brands choose to pursue more targeted users. One interesting example of this is the Nescafe Latino Facebook Community, which focuses on female Latinas in US. The community works around two main issues: Nescafe moments and the singer Ricky Martin.

Nescafe's Latino Facebook page, focuses on the female Latino community in the US.

Having a Facebook page centered around a brand will not immediately translate into a brand community. Many brands use social media, includingFacebook, specifically for brand interaction with custumers. This doesn't make this space a community. What makes an OBC a community is that even though the conversation is about or around the brand or the brand value, the OBC persists because of the interaction among the members (Brogi, 2014), and not just members' interaction with the brand. Four elements should be studied to determine the quality of an OBC:

1. Participation and interaction: As mentioned before, it is important to note not only the number of interactions with the brand but also the interactions among the members.

2. Quality of relationships within the community: How is the relationship between members? Is there any implicit social structure? Is there any antagonism?

3. Level of identification with the community: Do the members really feel like they are part of the community? Belongingness is one of the key issues in every type of community.

4. The quality of the communications: Between the users and with the brand, is the communication clear? What can be improved?

A new attempt to create a brand community may not rank well in the factors previously mentioned; a tight community will take some time to develop. At least three steps are essentials to consolidate a brand community (Rosenthal & Brito, 2017):

1. Topical information exchange: The brand community could begin as a virtual page that communicates information about the brand and discusses themes of interest with the audience.

2. Identity communication: As the OBC evolves, some specific signs of common identity should emerge and should be reinforced by the community administration. These signs can be: common codes or words that have a special internal meaning, and/or internal celebrities (people recognized as leaders inside the community) that influence the interactions with other members.

3. Own cultural norms: The OBC members feel a strong connection with the community. Common codes are easily shared between members that frequently interact, and internal celebrities are easily recognizable.

Influencer Marketing

One of today's trends in social media marketing is the use of influencers. A trend that started as sponsoring celebrities in social media now has evolved to include micro or even nano influencers. Different authors write about different categorizations of influencers; one possible categorization is size (Ruiz-Gómez, 2019):

- Mega-Influencers: Mega stars with over 1 million followers. In this list we need to recognize the mega-influencers who became influencers in social meda and the ones that are influencers for other reasons and now use social media as another platform.

Influencer marketing has become an important tool for many brands.

- Macro-Influencers: Between 100 thousand to 1 million followers, with high engagement.

- Micro-Influencers: Up to 100 thousand, with high engagement and usually a specific niche.

- Nano-Influencers: This could vary from very little but specific or local followers to less than 100 thousand followers. This type of influencers targets not only a specific audience but most of the time a specific theme.

Other categories are possible; for example, in HubSpot they talk about KOL, or Key Opinion Leaders, as highly specialized people in a specific field (Baker, 2019).

Some of the considerations that brands have to have when using influencer marketing are provided below:

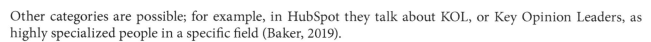

- Have a clear objective. Just because influencer marketing is a big trend, doesn't mean that it is for every brand. Brands need to decide if this is something in line with their strategy and IMC goals.

- Influencer marketing is not advertising. The content should be carefully crafted to look natural and honest (Hennessy, 2018).

- Brand alignment. The brand and the influencer identity must be aligneded. The organic (non-paid) content that the influencer posts must be naturally aligned with the brand, so the paid post doesn't feel forced (Idem). The motivation of the influencer also should be aligned with the brand motivations.

- Number of followers is not always key. The number of followers, even though important, is not the key element to deciding on an influencer. Some followers can be fake or even if real, if the influencer doesn't have a high engagement, the number of followers is not important.

- How to get Influencers. Today some specialized companies represent and recruit influencers. Some ad or communication agencies can also do this work. Another alternative is the use of apps or platforms to match influencers with brands.

- Disclose the relationship. The FTC has asked brands to clearly disclose brand relationships with influencers. This doesn't need to be an extremely long text; in fact, some type of #ad or #partnership hashtag would work. (Recommended Reading: FTC on Influencers Disclosure)

Growth Hacking/Marketing

Growth hacking, or growth marketing, is not a particular strategy for IMC in social media. It is not even a specific IMC strategy in general. However, as a buzzword in most startups and with a logic based on the same used in social media, we thought it important to at least mention it, especially because many technology companies today have a growth marketing director or a similar figure. Companies such as Google, Facebook, and DropBox are well-known companies that use this type of approach.

In theory, growth hacking, is just what the name says, how to hack growth, using creative, low-cost strategies,to accelerate the adoption of a specific offering. Many of the elements of growth hacking are not so different from what marketing should be. First, we should have a product market fit, then

A great example of growth hacking is Dropbox. They offered free space to users who successfully invited other users. They did this after carefully analyzing that most users were referrals from other users and not a product of the online advertising at the moment.

access to modifications in the entire supply change not only in the promotion/distribution segment. Finally, Growth hacking is completely data driven. Four steps are important in hacking growth (Ellis & Brown, 2017):

1. Analyze: Quantitative and qualitative data analysis must be done to understand potential opportunities for growth.

2. Ideate: Brainstorm ideas of hypothesis and market experiments to run.

3. Prioritize: Choose the most relevant and convenient experiments.

4. Test: Run the experiments and see what works; get back to step one.

The Future

So far we have discussed several different social media platforms and strategies; however, this world of technology is constantly evolving; marketers today need to begin to understand how the future of social media is changing. Some considerations are:

- AR and VR: Snapchat is already changing the landscape; however, we still need to see how immersive virtual reality is going to play out. Facebook spent millions of dollars buying and perfecting the Oculus Rift. We still haven't seen all the implications for marketing this technology.
- Artificial Intelligence: Chatbots is just one example of how AI can change the management and planning of social media.
- Internet of Things: As more and more artifacts are connected, the more insights and touchpoint opportunities we will have.
- Privacy concerns and limitations to targeting: This is an important discussion that will have implications on how far we go in the understanding of consumer insights.

Application Exercise:

Choose a brand and pick three social media platforms the brand is currently using; analyze.

Brand:			
Analyze	Platform 1	Platform 2	Platform 3
Platform			
Objective			
Audience			
Strategies in Use			
Other Comments			

References

Alton, L. (2017). 7 tips for creating engaging content every day. Retrieved from https://business.twitter.com/en/blog/7-tips-creating-engaging-content-every-day.html

Baker, K. (2019). The Ultimate Guide to Influencer Marketing in 2019. Retrieved from https://blog.hubspot.com/marketing/how-to-work-with-influencers

Berger, J. (2016). *Contagious: Why things catch on:* Simon and Schuster.

Brogi, S. (2014). Online Brand Communities: A Literature Review. *Procedia—Social and Behavioral Sciences, 109,* 385–389. http://dx.doi.org/10.1016/j.sbspro.2013.12.477

Ellis, S., & Brown, M. (2017). *Hacking Growth: How Today's Fastest-growing Companies Drive Breakout Success:* Currency.

Facebook. (2019). Facebook Company Info. Retrieved from https://newsroom.fb.com/company-info/

Hennessy, B. (2018). *Influencer: Building Your Personal Brand in the Age of Social Media:* Citadel.

Malhotra, A., Malhotra, C. K., & See, A. (2013). How to create brand engagement on Facebook. *MIT Sloan Management Review, 54*(2), 18.

Ramsaran-Fowdar, R. R. (2013). The Implications of Facebook Marketing for Organizations. *Contemporary Management Research, 9*(1), 73–84. doi:10.7903/cmr.9710

Rosenthal, B., & Brito, E. P. (2017). How virtual brand community traces may increase fan engagement in brand pages. *Business Horizons, 60*(3), 375–384.

Ruiz-Gómez, A. (2019). Digital Fame and Fortune in the Age of Social Media: A classification of social media influencers. *aDResearch ESIC: International Journal of Communication Research/ Revista Internacional de Investigación en Comunicación, 19*(19).

Smith, A., & Anderson, M. (2018). Social Media use in 2018. Retrieved from https://www.pewinternet.org/2018/03/01/social-media-use-in-2018/

Chapter 9
The Public Brand

The managing of the public discourse of the brand is an important part of IMC.

© wellphoto/Shutterstock.com

Communicating the brand is not limited to the market or the consumers; many other stakeholders are relevant in brand development. In this chapter, we discuss how to use public relations and what to do when the brand is under attack. In addition, the chapter goes over two other channels for the IMC arsenal: events and sponsorships and product placement.

Learning Objectives for This Chapter:

- Discuss the importance of different stakeholders for the brand.
- Distinguish the main elements in public relations.
- Be able to design a strategy to respond when the brand is under attack.
- Recognize the factors for a successful use of sponsorships and event marketing.
- Discuss the relevance and strategies of product placement.

The Brand in the Eye of the Public

So far, we have discussed the brand message and traditional advertising, the use of digital platforms, and the application of social media. But the choices for our IMC tool kit don't end there.

Until now, in this book, most of the communication has been from the brand directly to the target market. However, not all brand communications should be only to the potential buyer. Brands should pay attention to other groups of people as well. For example, a young couple having their first baby may be the target for a diaper brand. But other members of the community can be of significance in influencing the parents' decisions.

Other types of audiences can also be important; sometimes these are not always considered in marketing communications, but nevertheless they should be aligned with the IMC strategy. Communications can target internal clients, investors, policy makers, or local communities just to give a few examples. Most of these groups may not be direct consumers but they can be extremely crucial for most brands.

One of the tools that brands use to talk to a broad audience is Public Relations (PR); this is not to say that PR is exclusively for this type of communication, as PR can also be used for specific consumer targeting. However, PR has the ability to help us talk to a broader audience. We will discuss this use of PR at the beginning of this chapter.

Brands should consider not only talking to their target markets but also to a broad range of stakeholders.

© Microgen/Shutterstock.com

Sometimes brands make mistakes or they are accused of something negative. PR and other communication tools are extremely important to manage those types of situations. In the second part of this chapter, we will discuss how to react when the brand is under attack. This chapter will finish with other tools to create good feelings about the brand through events, sponsorships, and brand placement.

Managing Public Relations

Public Relations is defined as, "that form of communication management that seeks to make use of publicity and other nonpaid forms of promotion and information to influence the feelings, opinions, or beliefs about the company, its products or services, or about the value of the product or service or the activities of the organization to buyers, prospects, or other stakeholders" (AMA). A couple of things that you can read in this definition are very important. First, is that PR is a non-paid effort to appear in the media to influence a broad range of stakeholders. Also, its focus is to influence perceptions and emotions about the brand. Because it is non-paid, marketers should always remember that they are not dealing with advertising, so you cannot control what the press says about you; however, a good strategy would be to try to positively influence them.

Different companies use different methods to manage the PR responsibilities. Sometimes PR will be a part of the marketing department; sometimes it will be under the VP or director of communications; sometimes it can be its own department or even be managed by an outside agency. Each company has to decide what model suits them best and how relevant PR is for them.

PR can have many responsibilities, some of them are:

- Analyze and update the **internal and external stakeholders** of the company.
- **Monitor and evaluate** the corporate and brand media; this evaluation is both quantitative (as in number of pages, for example) and qualitative. The continuous monitoring of the press or clipping articles to detect when a brand or company is mentioned is of extreme importance in the management of the PR, brand building, and the anticipation of/response to a crisis.
- Evaluation of the **corporate reputation** among the different stakeholders and assessment of image risks of the company and brand.
- Generation **of strategy and tactics for earned media** presence through events, press releases, etc.
- Creating **good will** for the brand trough corporate social responsibility and/or cause marketing is also sometimes an important piece of PR.
- Prevent or reduce image damage in cases of **brand crisis**.

Two elements are key when working with PR for a brand: the press kit and press releases. Let's briefly discuss them.

The **press kit** or a media kit is a package with everything that the media might need to know about a brand. This should be given to the press at a specific event or be sent to them. Today, it is common for big companies to have a micro-site on their Website that contains press kit materials. Usually a press kit contains the following:

- A letter of introduction to the brand
- The brand or company story
- Various company facts
- A list of company officials
- Press releases
- Logos
- Images
- Any other relevant material

An important part of successful PR is writing **press releases**. These are direct communications from the brand to the press. Keep in mind that the press will decide if they want to publish the material or not. And even if they do, they could just publish a part of it. Always remember that the press will be the first target when you are writing a press release.

When creating a press release, the author should try to write a short but catchy headline, get to the point as soon as possible, and make the information included relevant to the audience. Some ideas that can help press releases to be more successful are (Craumer, 2002) :

- **Timeliness:** The media moves with publics agendas; the question here is if the press release is tied in with that agenda.
- **Relevance:** Does the press release have a specific relevance for the audience? Even though press releases from a brand are a marketing tool, they should not be about the brand specifically, but about the implications for the audience.
- **Proximity:** Is the release local or national? A local press release may find an easier path to being included in local news.
- **Prominence:** Is the brand a very well-known brand? Is a celebrity involved? The press will typically attempt to give more space to well-known actors even if the news is not so relevant.

- **Human interest:** Does it tell a human story? A touching story about a kid or a family that suffers specific consequences that others can relate to can impact thousands of people.
- **Rarity: Is it funny?** Is there something bizarre about your topic? It's called news because it might be something not necessarily seen or know before. The press tends to give space to things that are not common; there's a saying that when a dog bites a person, that is not news, but a human biting a dog will makes the news. This, of course, is just a metaphor, but it explains the spirit of what you want to show in PR.

A different approach to publishing news about the brand is responding to possible queries from a journalist. For this situation, the marketer will need to know when a journalist is looking for a story and pitch an angle to incorporate the brand. Often, this is possible when working with highly connected communications or PR agencies or professionals. For mid-size companies that may not have the needed network, services—for example, HARO (Help a Reporter Out)—are good alternatives.

To use HARO, marketers need to enroll in www.helpareporter.com and subscribe to the mailing list. Normally, HARO will send out three emails daily that can be divided by categories. Most of the time, responding to HARO is time sensitive, so the marketer must be sure to respond quickly. Also, keep in mind that your email is competing for the journalist's attention.

Press releases play an important role in IMC; however, don't expect that all your press releases will be published as is every time.

Application Exercise

Read the recommended article: "8 Ridiculous Examples of Press Release Fails." Then choose and evaluate a press release according to the variables previously discussed:

Timeliness:
Relevance:
Proximity:
Prominence:
Human Interest:

The Brand under Attack

Most brands at one time or another will face some type of a crisis. Sometimes it can be a minor issue; other times it might be a much bigger problem. Today's rea- time exposure of the brand can lead to many more possibilities of attack. Since 2009 when Dave Carrol made a song for United Airlines (Wilson, Zeithaml, Bitner & Gremler, 2012) because they broke his guitar, viral complaints in social media have become very popular.

Dave Carrol in 2009 created a viral video with a song for United Airlines.

Recommended Video: Dave Carrol at TED

Whatever the problem suggested by a video on YouTube, or a last-minute tweet, or a deep journalistic report published by national media, brands need to know when and how to respond. We will focus on how to answer attacks where the traditional media is involved, even if they started in digital channels.

One of the first decisions that a marketing team needs to make is when to respond and when not to respond. This is a delicate choice, as not responding when you should can lead to a bigger conflict. But sometimes responding when the crisis was going to be over soon may just put more fuel on the fire. The teams need to assess elements, such as how long might it be on the news, would more news come up about the situation or is it just this? Is there other news coming soon that may distract the attention of the public? Also, the relevance of the crisis is important—not just how big and important but how much is it tied to the core values of the brand? Whatever you decide, it is important to keep monitoring the situation.

When responding to a crisis situation, some of the things that the marketer needs to determine is whether this is a real transgression or not and how severe it is. According to these elements, the marketer or crisis team will likely want to influence the consumer perception of the crisis. Some of these perceptions to monitor are (Johar, Birk, & Einwiller, 2010):

- **True:** If it is not a real transgression, the brand will want to lower the perception of truth in the public mind.
- **Responsibility:** If it is a real transgression, the marketer will want the consumer to perceive it as something not (or at least not completely) a responsibility of the brand.
- **Intentionality:** As in the previous factor, the brand wants to be perceived as making a mistake and not involved in deliberate or planned wrongdoing.
- **Recurrence:** The brand wants to assure the audience that this is not something that will happen again.
- **Brand reflection:** Consider how the perception in the audience's mind can be influenced to separate (in part, at least) the event from the brand image.

Different strategies can be used to work on these perceptions; these strategies are divided mostly around whether the transgression is real or not, but you also have to consider the severity of the crisis and how engaged the consumers are with the brand (Johar et al., 2010).

Strategies for Real Transgressions

Come Clean: When the transgression is real and the crisis is severe, sometimes the only choice is to come clean as soon as possible. The brand will take a hit but it may still be able to move forward quickly. For real transgressions, if the company doesn't give all of the information soon, the risk is that more and more info will be leaked to the press and the time of the crisis can be extended.

Polish the Halo: This strategy is to be used together with the previous strategy discussed in very severe cases. The idea is to complement the "Come Clean" response with more branding efforts in advertising and events like cause marketing to give a stronger halo, or better image, to the brand. All these have to be done carefully so the brand doesn't appear to be trying to wash away the image or make an excuse for the damage.

Not Just Me: This is to be used in situations of real transgression when the company can show that the problem is more of an industry one or a more macro problem. This, however, has to be carefully executed.

Inoculation: This is the only strategy that has to be used before a crisis. Sometimes a brand has information that a crisis will hit and can prepare the terrain.

Yes…but: Similar to the "Come Clean" response, but focused on the less engaged consumers, in this strategy apart from telling the facts as soon as possible, the brand will explain with a lot ofd detail what generated the crisis.

Strategy for Not-Real Transgression

Rebuttal: If the transgression is not real, but could be perceived as severe, at least from the less engaged consumers, the brands will want to do a point-by-point rebuttal of the accusation.

Attack the Accuser: In certain cases when the attack is severe but not real, the company could try to attack the accuser. This strategy has to be used carefully as it can alienate less engaged consumers and could motivate a stronger counter-attack from the accuser.

No, Not I: When the crisis is not severe, not real, and we have a strong tie with our consumers, sometimes the best idea is just to generally deny the accusations without entering into deep discussions.

One important thing to consider is that these strategies are designed from a branding and communication point of view. It is, however, extremely important that the crisis committee seeks advice from a legal perspective before making any decisions on responses.

Sometimes, when the transgression is real, these strategies will require an apology from a company official. This apology has to be carefully crafted with a specific objective in mind. The five steps for an apology strategy are listed below (Clow & Baack, 2018):

1. Express guilt or regret.
2. Recognize the wrong behavior and acceptance of possible sanctions.
3. Reject of the inappropriate behavior.
4. State correct behavior and how the brand will engage in it in the future.
5. Explain the compensation or reparation that the brand will do because of the transgression.

Events and Sponsorships

One interesting way that some brands engage with consumers is by sponsoring events, teams, or people. This can be related to causes, arts, sports, or any other type of activity. However, for the most part, sporting events are what most brands use.

Event marketing is a very unique type of marketing; most of the time, it is a complete immersive experience that the audiences will live. Events can be targeted to specific lifestyles and psychographics. When a positive involvement of the consumer exists with the brand and with the event, it can impact sales. in this sense, a third driver is the fit between the brand and the event (Martensen, Grønholdt, Bendtsen & Jensen, 2007).

Energy drinks like Monster have a good fit with extreme sports and they have used this as an important part of their IMC strategy.

A well-commented controversy in event marketing is the concept of **ambush marketing**. This has been a problem in the last couple of Olympic Games. Ambush marketing is when a brand uses an event that they are not sponsoring to boost their own promotions. This could include anything from a small visual clue of the event to a more notorious element. The ethics of ambush marketing, or at least of the most aggressive versions, is an important discussion in IMC.

As with events, the fit between the sponsors, teams, or athletes with the brand, for example, is very important. In this case the brand and the person or group sponsored will act in a co-branding effect, where some the brand associations of one will affect the other. These include positive and negatives associations. This is why one of the risks of sponsorships is that the sponsored person or group could commit a transgression that may jeopardize the brand's value.

Brand Placement

Apart from sponsorship and events, two other types of brand partnerships can reach an audience without looking like advertising; these are: **brand placement** and **branded entertainment**.

The most known of these is brand placement where the brand is featured in a cultural product; these can be books, movies, TV shows, or games to name a few. Movies, however, are where most brand placements are occurring today.

Three primary strategies are used in product placement (Williams, Petrosky, Hernandez & Page Jr, 2011):

- Implicit product placement: The brand logo or the product itself is shown in the background or used for context but no particular attention is paid to the product.

- Integrated explicit product placement: The product or brand is not just mentioned but also plays a role in the scene and works to show the quality of the product. Many cars use this strategy. Lexus was used for a chase in the Black Panther movie; and Bumblebee, in the Transformers movie, was a Camaro.

- Non-integrated explicit product placement: The brand acts as a sponsor of the cultural product and it will be explicitly mentioned but will not be integrated in the storyline.

Brand entertainment is similar to brand placement; however, the complete story is around the brand. Examples of these are ad gaming like the one from Burger King where you can play with its "king," or Lego movies that revolve around the brand.

© Jeff Bukowski/Shutterstock.com

The partnership between Lexus and Marvel's Black Panther included a big car chase with a product placement of the car.

References

AMA. Public Relations Definition. *Marketing Dictionary*. Retrieved from https://marketing-dictionary.org/p/public-relations/

Clow, K., & Baack, D. (2018). *Integrated Advertising, Promotion, and Marketing Communications* (8 ed.).

Craumer, M. (2002). Why Your Press Releases Aren't Making News. *Harvard Management Communication Letter, 5*(1), 3.

Johar, G. V., Birk, M. M., & Einwiller, S. A. (2010). How to save your brand in the face of crisis. *Mit Sloan Management Review, 51*(4), 57.

Martensen, A., Grønholdt, L., Bendtsen, L., & Jensen, M. J. (2007). Application of a model for the effectiveness of event marketing. *Journal of Advertising Research, 47*(3), 283–301.

Williams, K., Petrosky, A., Hernandez, E., & Page Jr, R. (2011). Product placement effectiveness: Revisited and renewed. *Journal of Management and Marketing research, 7*, 1.

Wilson, A., Zeithaml, V. A., Bitner, M. J., & Gremler, D. D. (2012). *Services marketing: Integrating customer focus across the firm:* McGraw Hill.

Chapter 10
Selling the Brand

The purchase step sometimes requires a last push; this chapter covers the IMC components that are better suited for this.

© Harbucks/Shutterstock.com

Transforming brand equity into sales sometimes requires a last push. This final chapter goes into some of the IMC components that are more favorable for this push: database marketing, personal selling, direct response marketing, and sales promotions.

Learning Objectives for This Chapter:

- Differentiate the elements of database marketing.
- Discuss the importance of the role of customer relationship marketing.
- Distinguish the appropriate elements to integrate personal selling in the IMC strategy.

- Recognize examples of a direct response marketing campaign.
- Be able to decide when and how to use the different alternatives in consumer sales promotions.

Call to Action and Sales Conversion

As we have mentioned before, IMC strategy leads to brand equity. One of the objectives in many companies is the achievement of constant growth. This constant growth can be obtained by acquiring new clients, generating more value from current clients, generating a new use opportunity for our products, and more. It is, however, important to note that most of these cases require the consumer to buy something, so IMC and brand equity are, or should be, linked to sales generation.

In previous chapters, we have discussed some issues relevant to sales generation, such as, for example, calls to action in digital and social marketing, as well as in traditional advertising. Some IMC platforms, however, are more suited to boost sales conversion than others. In this chapter, we will examine four types of IMC channels that are designed to move a customer to action. This is not saying that these channels do not have a long-term brand development role, but their nature is closer to sales generation. The IMC channels that we will discuss are:

- Database marketing
- Personal selling
- Direct marketing
- Sales promotion

Database and the New Technology

We have discussed how new technology affects marketing in previous chapters. Our discussion has mainly revolved around social and digital media and how they help us communicate in a faster and more direct way with our customers. Through these, we can listen to what our customers say and micro-target them. However, the opportunity that technology brings to marketing goes further than those methods. In general, the ability to collect and manage consumer data in each touchpoint today is essential. This is where Database Marketing (DBM) comes into play, as a method that drives the company's customer acquisition on one hand and customer relations on another. When using DBM, brands can identify customers clustered by value for the company, forecast potential customer behavior, and make informed decisions (Guarda et al., 2018).

DBM is relevant for the complete IMC strategy and process. It, is, however, close to two of the IMC channels that we will discuss further in this chapter; these are personal selling ,as DBM should drive the sales and customer relationship process;, and direct response marketing, as this process will depend on customer data to be effective.

Some of the concepts that are relevant to understanding DBM are:

Data warehouse: With all of the diferent systems in which the company will attract data points, a data warehouse allows users to acces this data in an integrated platform. A data warehouse is a repository of all internal and external data for the company (Harmon, 2003).

Data mining: If the data warehouse is the memory, data mining is the intelligence (Berry & Linoff, 2004). Data minning is the process and tools to mine, or dig through, the data to understand and discover patterns that can be used for marketing decisions.

Customer Relationship Management (CRM): A concept that is close to DBM but from a distinct perspective is the concept of CRM. CRM as a concept has been gaining more traction over the years; it is, however, a term that can cause confusion. When executives or professionals talk about CRM, they can be doing it from three different perspectives (SalesForce):

- **A strategy:** A central business philosophy and decision guide that puts the customers at the center and/or interacts with them one on one.
- **A process:** A series of steps or a system to involve those relationships with customers.
- **A technology:** The technology that allowes the company to interact and record the interaction with customers.

SalesForce is one of the most used CRM systems today.

© Piotr Swat/Shutterstock.com

More than that, CRM should be a way to conduct business where the customer is at the center. In this manner, concepts, such as CLV and share of customers (see Chapter 5) are extremely important. At the formation stage of a Customer Relationship Management approach, companies should make three decisions (Parvatiyar & Sheth, 2001):

- The purpose and objectives of engaging in CRM
- The selections of the partners and customers that will be the focus of CRM
- The selection of the specific CRM programs

The Role of Sales in IMC

Traditionally, the IMC literature considers personal selling as a major component in IMC (Keller, 2016). Its many forms includes the likes of sales presentations, sales meetings, sales incentive programs, tradeshows, and more (IDEM).

However, in practice, the concept of personal selling as a component of IMC becomes more complicated. Not because a lack of importance, but by a lack of integration with marketing communications. Even further theory and practice shows that most of the time the marketing and sales relationship is a complicated one (Rouziès et al., 2005).

Personal selling is considered an important component in the IMC mix.

© fizkes/Shutterstock.com

Some authors have called the blend of marketing and sales as SMarketing (Hughes, Gray & Whicher, 2018). The integration of sales and marketing have been proven to have a positive impact on a company's performance (Rouziès et al., 2005). Some important considerations for a successful integration of the sales force and marketing include:

- **Common message and strategy:** As we have discussed throughout the entire book, all the touchpoints should deliver a consistent message. This is not the same as an identical message, but whatever the sales force says needs to be in line with all the other elements of IMC.
- **Objectives integration:** The sales force should have specific objectives that perfectly align with all the other company and marketing objectives. Also, all the parties involved should understand how they complement one another. Sometimes a short sight on sales goals can be seen as being antagonistic of a long-term brand creation by the different parties. These types of differences need to be discussed.

- **Leads definition:** A sales lead could be a person or organization that has the potential to become a customer. Leads can be obtained by companies in many ways—inbound or outbound—some of this lead generation can be obtained by advertising or improving the SEO or directly through the effort of the sales force. One problem that many companies face is the lack of definition of what constitutes a quality lead. So, marketing, for example, can obtain many leads that will be dismissed by sales. A good definition of what constitutes a good marketing-generated and/or sales-generated lead is crucial for better performance and a good relationship. Apart from a definition on the quality of a lead, sales and marketing should work hand in hand in the assessment and detection of new processes to generate leads.

- **Pipeline agreement:** The sales process doesn't end with lead generation. Most companies have or should have a definition, or map, of the entire pipeline. This is the entire process from detecting a potential opportunity to converting it to a lead, to establishign a loyal customer. Each company should define the exact stages of the pipeline. A good integration between sales and marketing needs to define what stages are the property of marketing and which stages are the property of sales.

- **Service-level agreement:** Some companies design and sign an internal service-level agreement to clearly define each role.

Other than good sales and marketing integration, brands need to decide on the role and relevance of personal sales in the IMC mix. Some companies will have a minimal sales force with most of their resources in other components, such as advertising or PR. In other cases, most of the IMC will be based around personal selling. Brands will use personal selling when the product and messages need some flexibility. In contrast to traditional advertising and PR, personal selling allows a salesperson to customize the message, price, and some of the features of the product to each customer. Other elements, like the timing and relationship with the clients, also favor of personal selling. It is, however, a method with (in general) a higher cost-per-contact, and that is difficult or costly to implement when the target is more geographically dispersed.

Direct Response Marketing

Another IMC component that is tied in with DBM is direct response marketing, , better known simply as direct marketing. The marketing dictionary defines this concept as the "the total of activities by which the seller, in effecting the exchange of goods and services with the buyer, directs efforts to a target audience using one or more media (direct selling, direct mail, telemarketing, direct-action advertising, catalog selling, cable selling, etc.) for the purpose of soliciting a response by phone, mail, or personal visit from a prospect or customer"(AMA).

As we can read in the definition, two elements are essential. First is specifically a target; this is where a correct use of database information is important to decide who to send direct marketing to; and second, it is to solicit some kind of response from the customer. Because of the high level of customization that is possible, normally direct marketing allows the marketer to be very creative on the design of the instrument; however, the strategy and search for effectiveness in the response is what matters the most.

As we discussed previously in Chapter 7, permission marketing is important, as unsolicited marketing has less impact than that which is solicited.

Some examples of direct marketing include (Clow & Baack, 2018):

- Direct mail with advertising sent to the target
- Catalogs mailed to the target
- Mass media that stimulates the instant response, such as "call now" infomercials
- Internet and e-mail direct marketing, as explained in Chapter 7
- Out-bound telemarketing call centers call customers to get an immediate response

Sales Promotions

Finally, we have our last, but no less important, IMC component to discuss: sales promotions. Sales promotions are IMC methods that look for an immediate response; they can be divided into consumer sales promotions and trade promotions that target members of the distribution channel (Blattberg & Neslin, 1990). To end this chapter, we will focus on consumer sales promotions.

We can distinguish at least two categories of consumer sales Promotion: monetary and non-monetary promotions (Chandon, Wansink & Laurent, 2000). The first one is the most common one as, for example, coupons and discounts. For non-monetary examples, we can look to games or premiums.

Consumer sales promotions can act on three levels (Yeshin, 2006):

- Communication: When well-done, a consumer sales promotion can deliver the right message, getting the consumer's attention at the point of sales.
- Incentive: They can offer some form of incentive for the consumer.
- Advance the decision: In a consumer's consideration to buy, sales promotions can help make the move from the thought of a purchase to a purchase decision faster.

The marketer should make the decision of implementing or not implementing sales promotions very carefully and with a specific objective in mind. Sales promotions can have many disadvantages or risks and also can be costly for the company. For example, some monetary sales promotions can encourage the consumer to buy only when there is a promotion. In this case, consumers will buy only if

Coupons are a popular method for monetary consumer sales promotions.

© Shmelkova Nataliya/
Shutterstock.com

they get a discount or have a coupon. Some literature sustains that a good portion of consumers would have bought the brand without the sales promotions, so the company is losing out. Another risk with sales promotions is the potential damage to the brand image; this is especially important for luxury brands, for example.

When planning sales consumer promotions, the marketer has to keep in mind that not all people and all segments react in the same way to sales promotions. Not only that, but the same person might react differently to sales promotions depending on the product category. This is how the same person, for example, will be a brand loyalist for shoes but will buy food according to the coupons that he or she possesses. Using the same perspective, some consumers will be more prone to buy when monetary incentives are the drivers of the promotion while others are more interested when non-monetary incentives are at stake. An example of the last one is kids that will plead with their parents to buy a cereal that has a small toy in the box.

A toy in the box—premiums are another popular consumer sales promotion.

© urbanbuzz/Shutterstock.com

Many different methods can be considered brand promotions, such as: coupons, discounts or price-offs, bonus packs, premiums, sweepstakes and contests, samplings, loyalty programs, and refunds and rebates (Blakeman, 2014). In the next table, we discuss the use of each of these:

Consumer Sales Promotions	Descriptions	Considerations
Coupons	A ticket that can be redeemed for a discount or another type of consumer benefit.	Many variations of coupons exist; they can be defined by the type of distribution, such as in-mail, electronically, in-store, or in-package; or how they can be used, such as instant redemption, buy back, or used to buy a different product (Crossruffing).
Discounts or Price-Offs	A "sale" where a particular price discount exists in the brand.	Can be an important driver of sales but can damage the brand if not used correctly.
Bonus Packs	Giving the consumer more products for the same price.	Can be used for adding value without lowering the price.
Premiums	A gift that is given to the consumer for buying a certain brand.	Premiums can be attractive as non-monetary promotions that add value for the consumer.
Sweepstakes and Contests	Games that involve the consumer with the brand. Sweepstakes are games of chance while contests are games of skills.	Today, sweepstakes and contests can drive people to interact with the brand and generate data. The marketer has to consider legal potential and legal requirements of sweepstakes and contests.
Sampling	Free products give the consumer an opportunity to try the offering.	Sampling are good drivers of new consumers and can be used in many ways as in-store, digitally, in-mail, or in media (e.g.: perfumes in magazines).
Loyalty Programs	Programs that reward the consumer for each buy in the form of points or other incentives.	These programs look to generate loyalty and growth in the customer share average. They can be complex membership-based programs or more simple continuity programs where the consumer gets rewards after each buy.
Refunds and Rebates	Money back to the consumer for buying something.	Most of the time, these will require some extra action from the consumer and can be hard to redeem. Rebates are frequently used in the car industry.

Many other methods can be applied in sales promotions, but those described above are the most relevant ones. As with any other IMC component, the decision of which one (or ones) to use will depend on the global strategy and how the component integrates with the other media in use.

Application Exercise

Choose a Brand and observe the brand for a week; then respond:

Brand:	
Name Three Types of Consumer Sales Promotion Used by the Brand:	
Consumer Sales Promotion	Objective (Why do you think the brand is using that type of sales promotion?)

References

AMA. Direct Marketing Definition. *Marketing Dictionary*. Retrieved from https://marketing-dictionary.org/d/direct-marketing/

Berry, M. J., & Linoff, G. S. (2004). *Data mining techniques: For marketing, sales, and customer relationship management:* John Wiley & Sons.

Blakeman, R. (2014). *Integrated Marketing Communication: Creative Strategy from Idea to Implementation:* Rowman & Littlefield.

Blattberg, R. C., & Neslin, S. A. (1990). Sales promotion. *Englewood Cliffs.*

Chandon, P., Wansink, B., & Laurent, G. (2000). A benefit congruency framework of sales promotion effectiveness. *Journal of Marketing, 64*(4), 65–81.

Clow, K., & Baack, D. (2018). *Integrated Advertising, Promotion, and Marketing Communications* (8 ed.).

Guarda, T., Augusto, M. F., León, M., Pérez, H., Torres, W., Orozco, W., & Bacilio, J. (2018). *Marketing Knowledge Management Model.* Paper presented at the International Conference on Information Theoretic Security.

Harmon, R. (2003). Marketing information systems. *Encyclopedia of information systems, 3*(1), 137–151.

Hughes, T., Gray, A., & Whicher, H. (2018). *Smarketing: How to Achieve Competitive Advantage Through Blended Sales and Marketing:* Kogan Page Publishers.

Keller, K. L. (2016). Unlocking the power of integrated marketing communications: How integrated is your IMC program? *Journal of Advertising, 45*(3), 286–301.

Parvatiyar, A., & Sheth, J. N. (2001). Customer relationship management: Emerging practice, process, and discipline. *Journal of Economic & Social Research, 3*(2).

Rouziès, D., Anderson, E., Kohli, A. K., Michaels, R. E., Weitz, B. A., & Zoltners, A. A. (2005). Sales and marketing integration: A proposed framework. *Journal of Personal Selling & Sales Management, 25*(2), 113–122.

SalesForce. What is CRM? Retrieved from https://www.salesforce.com/eu/learning-centre/crm/what-is-crm/

Yeshin, T. (2006). *Sales promotion:* Cengage Learning EMEA.

Lightning Source UK Ltd.
Milton Keynes UK
UKHW032200230821
389358UK00005B/329